The Teddy Bear Catalog

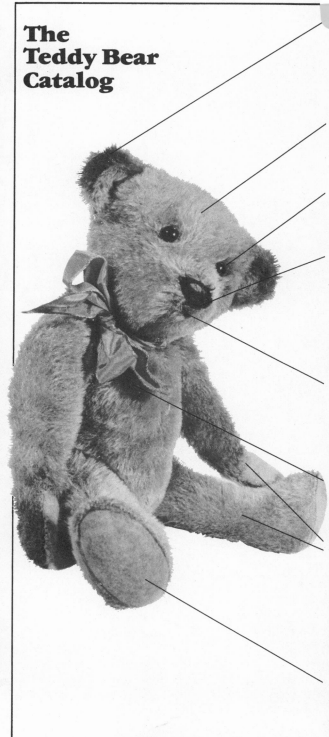

...a Teddy Bear's appendages, ears are often subjected to rough treatment and misused as handles.

Brain: Teddy Bear brains are remarkable for remembering only good things.

Eyes: Shoe buttons, buttons, glass stickpins, plastic, and thread are often used as eyes.

Nose and Mouth: Many bears start out with embroidery thread noses and mouths that are eventually worn away after years of serious cuddling and snuggling.

Voice: A bear's voice does not determine its sex. Teddy Bears are asexual. A deep voice indicates a "growler," a high voice, a "squeaker."

Heart: While invisible, the heart encompasses the entire torso of the Teddy.

Arms and Legs: Jointed limbs are preferred. Joints prevent torn ligaments and breakage. They also make it easier for bears to wave out of car windows.

Paws: Even when seriously damaged they still retain the ability to hold the smallest hands.

The Teddy Bear Catalog

Prices,
Care and
Repair,
Lore,
100s of
Photos.

Peggy and
Alan
Bialosky

Workman
Publishing
New York

Cover Teddy Bear:

See page 105,
Rare Bear Pair

Library of Congress Cataloging in Publication Data

Bialosky, Peggy.
    The Teddy bear catalog.

    1. Teddy bears—Collectors and collecting—Catalogs.
I. Bialosky, Alan, joint author.   II. Title.
NK8740.B5   688.7′24   80-51616
ISBN 0-89480-133-3

Cover Design: Paul Hanson
Book Design: Florence Cassen Mayers
Illustrations: Susan Gaber
Photographs: Marvin M. Greene
Additional Photographs: Peggy and Alan Bialosky, Stephen Butler
Special thanks to the following for use of their photographs in *The Teddy
Bear Catalog:* Kay Bransky, page 55; R. Dakin & Co., Pandas, page 23;
Don/Fagan International, Reuge Bear, page 189 and German Singing Bear,
page 197; Ideal Toy Corp., all photos page 16; Cecil St. Clair King, page 34;
Merrythought Ltd, Beefeater, page 124; Princess Soft Toys, Treasure Bear,
page 194; Margarete Steiff GmbH, Margarete Steiff, page 17 and "Jackie,"
page 26; *The Washington Post*, page 12 and page 14.

Workman Publishing Company, Inc.
1 West 39 Street
New York, New York 10018

Manufactured in the United States of America
First printing October 1980

10 9 8 7 6 5

Dedication To David, Jeff, and Randy

Acknowledgments The authors gratefully and warmly thank and
acknowledge the special people who helped
with the research and preparation of this book.
With deep appreciation, their most sincere
gratitude goes to:

Marvin M. Greene and

Dorothy Bordeaux; Ethel Boros; Kay Bransky;
Edson J. Brown and Ross Trump, Brown-Trump
Farm; Stephen A. Butler; Elsie Carper, *The
Washington Post;* Susan Critchfield, *The
Washington Post;* Gerald Fisher; Ed Freska; Pat
Garthoeffner, Toy Box Antiques; Helene Greene;
Tracy Greene; Rosalie Higgins and Randy Palmer,
Knickerbocker Toy Co., Inc.; Ideal Toy
Corporation; Ruth Kalb; Emily St. Clair King;
Roland M. Kraus; B.F. Michtom; Hilda Nieman;
Bob and Jackie Olson; Jan Pitney; Don and Mary
Jane Poley, Mary Jane's Dolls; Suzanne Rafer;
Kathy Goldblatt and Ruth Rashman, Rashman∕
King; Reeves International, Inc.; Zeke Rose,
Porter, Le Vay & Rose, Inc.; Bonnie Rowlands; Dr.
Mark Rutman; Klee Sherwood; John Shook; Hans
Otto Steiff; Margarete Steiff GmbH; Rose Vargo;
The White Elephant Sale of Cleveland, Ohio;
Barbara Wolters.

The Teddy Bear Catalog

Contents

Teddy Bear Price Guide

Directory

Why Teddy Bears?

What is it about a Teddy Bear? Since this century was very young, these warm, cuddly, special toys have been comforting boys and girls, as well as adults, through difficult years and trying times.

Similarly, Teddy Bears have been sharing happy occasions: birthdays, vacations, Christmas mornings, family reunions, and even college graduations. Why?

In our childhood, Teddy Bears are warm companions—good listeners, never critical, always reassuring. They are bear-shaped security blankets, huggable enough to fold in our arms, a perfect fit for our laps.

For adults, Teddy Bears are symbols of nostalgia, sort of furry Peter Pans that allow a very small part of each of us to remain a child forever. Could anyone ask for a more devoted friend?

Now our old friends have become extremely collectible. *The Teddy Bear Catalog* has been compiled by utilizing our own experience in collecting and by comparing the additional opinions of other collectors, dealers, and authorities over a geographically distributed area. The purpose of this book is to give readers a general idea as to the background and value of Teddy Bears. The prices noted are to be used as a suggested guideline.

Prices are rising. Values listed here are based on the market at the time this book was published. Prices will vary, depending upon a Teddy Bear's size, condition, appeal, and quality. Where sets are shown, the price as a complete set will exceed that of the sum of the prices for the individual pieces.

While every effort has been made to be accurate, the authors and publisher are neither liable nor responsible in any way for any errors in prices, information, and identification of the bears.

We sincerely hope you and your bears will enjoy this volume as much as we have enjoyed compiling it.

Scooter Bear
(See page 69)

The Teddy Bear Catalog

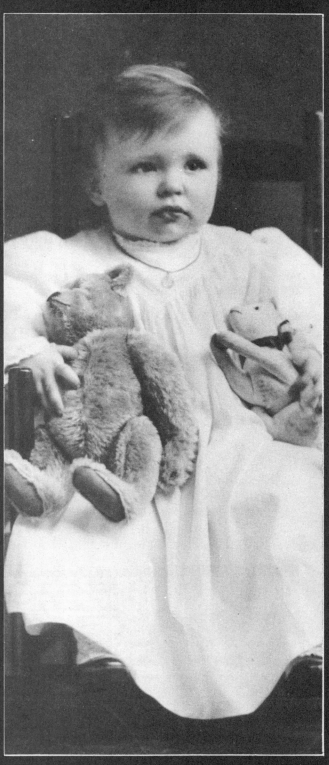

Even in the early 1900s, Teddy Bears accompanied children during photographic sessions.

Bear Beginnings

The actual "creation" is clouded in controversy. But, once upon a time (in 1902), one way or another, the Teddy Bear was born.

Teddy, to his friends

You see, it all started this way: President Theodore Roosevelt refused, while on a hunting trip, to shoot a captured bear. Many available accounts, including the popular retellings of the story, report the bear was a cub who either went on to live at the White House; at a Washington zoo; in a hotel with a handler; as a pet with relatives of the president; or as the mascot of the hunting camp, depending on which version of the story you read.

A few versions also state the bear wasn't a cub at all, but a weak, older bear.

Curious about the discrepancies, we began to do some research. It seemed important to get to the bottom of at least some of the mystery surrounding the Teddy's earliest beginnings. What we found (with the help of *The Washington Post*) is like finding there is no Santa Claus, or Tooth Fairy, or Easter Bunny—because it appears there really was no cute little bear cub.

Another myth up in smoke or No, Virginia . . .

On Saturday, November 15, 1902, the hunting incident, as it actually happened, was related in a front-page story in the *Post,* with a Mississippi dateline. The report was headlined, "One Bear Bagged," and further read, "But It Did Not Fall A Trophy To President's Winchester."

The Washington Post story that ran on November 15, 1902, related the hunting incident that initiated the creation of the original American "Teddy's Bears."

The detailed story goes on to explain that part of the president's hunting party trailed, then came upon, a lean, black bear (about 235 pounds). The exhausted animal was followed by the hunting dogs to a water hole. Desperate, the bear turned on the dogs, and even though it was "too exhausted to put up much of a fight," it managed to grab one of the hounds by the neck and kill it.

As the cornered bear made a swipe at another of the dogs, one of the men in the hunting party "knocked the game over with a blow on the head," probably with a rifle. "Then he blew his horn that the quarry had been brought to bay." A messenger was sent to bring back the president. Meanwhile, the bear was roped and tied to a tree. When Roosevelt arrived at the scene and saw the bear tied that way, "he would neither shoot it nor permit it to be shot."

"Put it out of its misery," he is reported to have said to one of the men. Subsequently, the hunter "ended its [the bear's] life with his knife."

Summing up the incident, the *Post* read: "President Called After the Beast Had Been Lassoed, but Refused to Make an Unsportsmanlike Shot."

But this is not the end of the story. On the following day, November 16, 1902, the refusal to shoot the bear became immortalized. It was coupled to a political incident related to a political dispute between Mississippi and Louisiana, and depicted in a cartoon by Clifford Berryman.

On November 16, the cartoon appeared on the front page of the Sunday *Post* as part of a montage titled, "The Passing Show." It shows Roosevelt, gun before him with its butt resting by his right foot. His back is to a plain, unhappy, *full-grown bear* with a rope around its neck, and Roosevelt is gesturing that he refuses to shoot the animal. Written across the lower portion of the cartoon are the words: "Drawing the Line in Mississippi." The cartoon received immediate and overwhelming attention.

But this is not the cartoon people are familiar with today. The one most often reprinted also has a 1902 date to the right of the signature. If you look closely, you will notice that this cartoon shows a smaller bear which seems more cub-like and appears to be shaking with fright. If you study the drawing, you will also notice that the president's rifle is resting more toward his left foot. In the *Post* cartoon, the President has two visible pockets on his jacket; there is only one visible in the other. The "shivering cub" cartoon is usually credited to *The Washington Star* and when Berryman left the *Post* he did indeed work for the *Star*; but that was after 1902 (he joined the *Star* in 1907), so the *Post* cartoon has to be the one which first appeared in print. During his career with the *Star*, Berryman included his by then famous bear in many of his cartoons— perhaps with each new rendering, it became more and more cub-like.

Opposite page:
The original Clifford Berryman cartoon as it appeared in *The Washington Post*, November 16, 1902. Although it may be difficult to tell in reproduction, the bear in this version is not shivering and has an obstinate, rather than scared, look on its face.

The more familiar Berryman cartoon attributed to *The Evening Star*. The bear has definitely taken on a more cub-like appearance, from its cute, helpless face, down to its quivering little body.

Enter the Michtoms

The American Teddy Bear's creators, Rose and Morris Michtom.

Despite what is probably the true nature of the hunting incident, and the look of the bear in Berryman's first cartoon, they both really seem to have triggered the birth of America's favorite stuffed toy, because subsequently, back in Brooklyn, New York, another event was taking place. Aware of all the attention the hunting incident and cartoon had attracted, Morris Michtom, a shopkeeper, displayed two toy bears in the window of his stationery and novelty store.

His wife, Rose Michtom, had made these bears: light-colored plush, stuffed with excelsior, and finished off with black shoe button eyes.

Looking at the two toy bears, Morris Michtom had a brilliant idea: he sought and received permission from President Roosevelt himself to call the new toys "Teddy's Bears."

An original 1903 Ideal Teddy Bear, one of which is in the Smithsonian in Washington, D.C.

The Michtoms' appealing plush bears became an overwhelming success. As they were sold, new ones were made, and by 1907 the demand was so great that the Michtoms moved their store to a loft as the Ideal Novelty and Toy Company.

Through the years, we have been fortunate enough to have had many conversations with B.F. Michtom, son of Ideal's famous founders and himself a retired chief of the company. "It is hard to determine manufacturers of Teddy Bears made from 1903 to 1910 or so, as brands were not stressed in those days," he told us. "But practically all bears made in this country from 1903 to 1906 were made by Ideal. Thereafter much competition set in, and probably no one alive now can identify exactly the manufacturer. Most bears were fully jointed: heads, arms, and legs turned. These were made mostly by either Ideal when domestically manufactured, or by Steiff when imported."

Steiff on the scene

About the same time that the Teddy Bear was created in the United States, it was also born in Germany.

The Steiff Company there, known for its unusually fine-quality stuffed animals, also made a wonderful stuffed bear toy during this historic 1902-1903 period.

Actually, the company's first stuffed toys weren't bears at all, but little wool-felt pincushion-type elephants. These were the original creations of Margarete Steiff, born in Giengen in 1847. During her childhood she fell victim to polio, which left her legs paralyzed and weakened her right hand. She wished to be independent and capable of earning her own living, and overcame her handicap by learning to sew. She offered the

Margarete Steiff pictured with one of her Teddy Bears.

stuffed elephants to the neighborhood children, who were delighted with them.

The little elephants were so popular that larger and different animals followed: a donkey, a horse, a pig, and even a camel.

It just so happened that Margarete's nephew, Richard Steiff, was an artist who had an interest in bears; he had spent time sketching brown bears in local zoos. Collaborating with his aunt, he influenced the development of a little jointed mohair bear toy. This new creation was exhibited at the 1903 Leipzig Fair in Germany. Its debut there created no great stir until the last

day of the fair: an American buyer noticed it, obviously had faith in it, and ordered several thousand of the little bears.

According to Steiff authorities, early Steiff bears were used as table decorations at the wedding festivities of President Roosevelt's daughter. Teddy Roosevelt was so enthusiastic about the bears, say the Steiff people, that the assemblage referred to them as Teddy-Bears.

At any rate, in 1903, a total of 12,000 of the items were made by the company; in 1907, that amount was 974,000. That's what you call a Teddy Bear boom.

Members of the classes of 1905-1907, pictured at their recent Teddy University class reunion. The three in the middle, of course, were on the football team.

The Steiff company was soon spoken of as the bear factory in Giengen, so the bear's head became the symbol used on all Steiff labels. The metal button in the ear was added as an additional trademark label during these years — and is still, of course, used today.

Also rans There are other tales as to the origin of the Teddy Bear including one from British bear fanciers who theorize that a member of royalty visiting the London Zoo might have conceived the idea. The Ideal and Steiff claims, however, are the two generally accepted by most people.

During the years that followed Teddy Bear development, innumerable Teddy Bear-related items appeared on the market: postcards, books (especially Teddy B and Teddy G: The Roosevelt Bears series written by Seymour Eaton, whose real name was Paul Piper), paper dolls, bears with light-up eyes, bear clothes, bear trunks and cases to keep the clothes in, bears to ride on automobiles, bear dishes to use for children's tea parties, bears that made noises or did tricks or were made as ornaments to adorn their owners. You name it, and it probably came decorated with a bear.

One of the early popular Roosevelt Bears adventure stories by Seymour Eaton (the pseudonym for Paul Piper.)

As the years passed, the Teddy Bear craze leveled off, but the Teddy Bear has remained a favorite toy, with millions sold yearly. Older bears and items related to them have now become collectors' treasures, and many of them are of extremely high value, both in the nostalgia they exude and in the amount of money they command. Some of the more unusual and appealing examples of this hobby are shown in the pages of this book.

An early photo of the author and her original bear friend. Separated sometime in her youth, the author has spent years of her life trying to relocate her bear. Pleads the author, "Teddy come home."

Bear Hunting

Want some advice on how to hunt down and buy a bear? If you are a beginning collector it is best to start by becoming familiar with and collecting new (modern) bears, for a number of reasons. New bears still wear their original tags and are bought from retail dealers. That means there is no great risk. You know exactly what you're getting: the name of the manufacturer, the stuffing and covering materials, and the name, if any, of the particular model.

New bears

Potentially collectible new bears of adequate quality frequently sell anywhere from ten dollars up, and are often in the fifteen to thirty-five dollar range. (High quality and prestige-brand bears may sell at higher prices). Since old Teddy Bears are far more costly, you can limit your financial risk by investing in a new one.

Furthermore, you can take your time selecting a new bear. Since other buyers aren't competing against you, you have time to think about the toy, knowing it will probably still be available the next day. Bears in limited editions or from close-out stock, of course, present a more pressured situation, but it is still not as competitive as the antique bear market. And buying from an established business means that if you decide the bear purchase is not really what you want or that it is defective, you can exchange or return it.

Making decisions

But which bear should you buy, and how do you select one? Generally it is best to pick a bear that is durable. If the arms and legs are jointed, is the bear made well enough so that those joints will not separate? Does the head swivel? Many youngsters try to turn the heads on their bears, and if that part of the anatomy is not jointed, the result can be, at the very least, a whiplash injury.

Keep in mind that many bears that are not jointed are still of fine quality. The important thing to look for is that it is not overstuffed, which puts too much stress on the seams. This can lead to frequent repairs and an unsatisfactory toy.

Once you have decided on the bear model, pick a cute face. Study all the expressions and choose one you really think has appeal. If you have to order by mail or phone, state on your order: "Please pick out one with a really appealing expression." Don't be embarrassed; after all, you're the one who is paying for it.

No matter how many identical bears a company makes, if you study a store display, you'll see no two look exactly alike. Some even have crooked eyes, pushed-in noses, lopsided ears. Check the bear over carefully, and if you're not sure, don't buy anything.

Character bears

Many collectors become interested in character bears: Yogi Bear; Smokey the Bear; the Disney bears, to name a few. While characters are a separate category by themselves, they are still considered by most collectors to be versions of a Teddy Bear and are sought after as such. Pandas and Koalas are also purchased by some collectors, although a great many don't consider them Teddy Bears. Kissing cousins, maybe.

Some Teddy Bear collectors develop a passion for pandas even though they aren't Teddies.

Koalas in your Teddy collection? Why not?

One character bear particularly in vogue is Dakin's "Misha," which was originally tied in with the 1980 Moscow Olympics. Because there was controversy over the event itself, and because the little stuffed bear's fate was widely publicized, it is now a natural for the true collector in its original form, which includes a detachable Olympic belt. Misha has been redesigned to sell dressed in a T-shirt, without the belt and comes in assorted sizes and styles.

Fozzie Bear, the beloved Muppet, is another example of a collectible character with endearing qualities.

Possum Trot's "UFB" (Unidentified Flying Bear) and Barbara Isenberg's "Running Bear" are bears we like for future possibilities because they are particularly timely items, being representatives of the space age (the former) and of our passion for physical fitness (the latter).

Rock-A-Bye-Baby, Inc.'s "Rock-A-Bye-Bear" is also a good bet to become a collectible. This toy includes a battery-operated mechanism which makes prenatal sounds designed to soothe and relax infants. Keep in mind that in many cases this type of toy is only valued as collectible if the mechanism is kept in working condition.

Dakin's "Misha"

Princess Soft Toys puts out a variety of real
charmers, some even dressed in colorful clothes;
Freemountain Toys makes "Emile Bearheart,"
quite unique looking: complete with two pockets
and a stuffed red heart. Another "hearty" fellow
is made by Enesco and also holds a stuffed red
heart.

Freemountain's Emile
Bearheart is unusual and
100% Teddy.

Commemorative bears

Any bear tied in with a commemorative event is a good prospect for collectors. Steiff's two anniversary bears are naturals. Jackie is the bear Steiff put out in 1953, commemorating the fiftieth anniversary of its Teddy (first made in 1903). Originally it had a tag with the name "Jackie" and the fiftieth anniversary information, but these tags often fell off when children played with the toys.

Steiff's "Jackie."

The new Steiff commemorative bear (marking the company's 100th year) is a reproduction of the company's first Teddy and has been available in a limited edition about $150. It is fully jointed, of fine quality, appealing, and will be sought after and highly prized. If you already own one, you are lucky; if not, have fun treasure-hunting: it will most likely increase in value and make you happy you splurged.

Steiff's anniversary bear commemorating the company's 100th year.

Only 11,000 of these bears were produced for worldwide sales: 5,000 have certificates in English, 4,750 of which were distributed by Reeves, International of New York. Fifty were held for specials and 200 were distributed in other English-speaking countries.

Six thousand remaining Teddy Bears have certificates in German; some of these have undoubtedly found their way into the American market. The certificates on all 11,000 collectibles have been signed by Hans Otto Steiff, head of the company, and they have been numbered: 1-6,000 for the German edition; 1-5,000 for the English.

Ideal's 1978 Teddy Bear was produced for that company's seventy-fifth birthday edition of its own original Teddy. The colorful accompanying box tells the history of the toy and has "Collector's Edition" printed across the front. This item would be very nice in a beginner's collection. It is a really appealing toy and can still be found if you scout around a little.

The bear Ideal issued commemorating its Teddy Bear's 75th anniversary.

Premiums and foreign bears

Any bear that is very well made, particularly appealing, and a little bit different has a good chance of increasing in value. This includes bears offered as premiums, naturals for the beginning collector. Chase Manhattan Bank, Snow Crop, Travelodge, and Avon have offered attractive bears.

Foreign-made new bears are also desirable among collectors, even if they are regular line bears which are not produced for one special occasion. Italy's Lenci, England's Merrythought and Peggy Nisbet, Germany's Hermann (as well as Steiff), and Käthe Kruse are but a few. Look around: you'll find more. Be prepared to spend a little extra though; these bears can sell for well over thirty-five dollars.

TEDDY BEAR PARTY
FEED THE TEDDY BEAR

Party goers in 1907 enjoyed a bear game similar to Pin the Tail on the Donkey. This one has players feeding the berries to the bear.

Put a British bear on your shelf. These are two from Merrythought, one old (left), the other modern.

Check in the New Bear section of this catalog for photos of some bears which we believe will soon become collectibles. The manufacturers and importers source list on page 214 gives company addresses if you would like to write for catalogs or other information.

Now, let's go on to antique and other collectible bears. First, what are they? While some purists feel antiques are things that are one hundred years old or older, today's bear collectors don't adhere to that rule. In the first place, how could they? The Teddy Bear was only born in the early 1900s.

Veteran bear hunters usually consider bears made before 1940 antiques. Bears made after that date, but discontinued or changed in style may also become valuable and sought as collectibles. Both types are becoming difficult to find and expensive to buy. As more and more people are drawn to the magic of Teddy Bears, these items continue to increase in value. The best part of collecting them is that they exude their own special charm and charisma.

Many collectors like to specialize. Some prefer Teddies that are six inches or under. Others buy only giants. Some bearaholics want the jointed types or mechanicals. Others insist their bears be

Antique bears

The long and the short of bear collecting.

covered only in mohair. Many collect bears produced by certain companies: Steiff, Ideal, Chad Valley, Schuco, and Shackman are among the more popular manufacturers of collectibles. Many people have enormous collections, sometimes three or four hundred bears. We know of one collection which contains 1,200. Don't let that throw you. A friend of ours has fewer than a dozen but they are of fine quality and in superb condition. Hers is one of the finest collections we've seen.

The hunt is on

But where do you, as a collector, find rare bears? Flea markets, house sales, auctions, antique and doll repair shops, house or garage sales, basements or attics, resale shops—even trash cans (don't laugh! We've done it).

A wonderful lady in England wrote us about an old bear her husband found lying in the middle of the street, possibly dropped from some passing car. Luckily for her, he rescued it, and it was a beauty. Lucky for that bear, too, of course.

Antique bears also show up at charity bazaars, rummage sales, and even in lost-and-found boxes at shopping centers, public stadiums, and arenas: anywhere lost mittens, boots and sweaters live. Scout around. Use your ingenuity; half the fun is in the searching.

Visit local stores that specialize in Teddy Bears and other antiques. Familiarize yourself with the feel and look of older bears. Find out as much as you can about the background of each bear from the retailer. Any information a knowledgeable retailer is willing to impart helps you in developing expertise in the field, and it will come in very handy when you are confronted with a labelless, seemingly unidentifiable flea market bear.

If you don't know of any stores to visit, consult the retailers list in the directory, page 217. Each listing includes an address and telephone number. If none are close by, write the retailers who are closest. Perhaps they know of other shops or private collectors near you.

Once you find a rare bear why not display it in a rare setting. This one sits in a unique old French goat cart.

Also consider joining a Teddy Bear club and subscribing to several hobby magazines and newsletters. These will keep you informed as to current prices, put you in touch with other collectors, and keep you posted as to current bear-related events. Check the directory, pages 220 and 221 for the names of clubs and publications.

If you are having trouble finding old bears, try running a "Wanted To Buy" classified advertisement in any newspaper or collectible-related magazine. Typical ads for this purpose might read as follows:

Try advertising

Wanted to buy—Old Teddy Bears in good condition from 1950 or earlier.

Or: Cash paid for Teddy Bears at least thirty years old. Related items also wanted.

(Related items can be clothes, dishes, prints, books, jewelry, almost anything.)

If you see a bear you feel is irresistible or that is part of a set of which you already own another part, buy it. Otherwise, if it is a rare bear or in good condition, by the time you think about it and come back it will have been long gone.

On the other hand, if you happen onto a bargain but don't really like the bear, it's not a bargain. Don't buy it. Learn to trust your instincts.

There are collectors who specialize in Teddy Bear postcards. This is an early example.

Bear alert What should you look for? The cream of the crop. Mohair, if you're lucky. Mohair was a term usually applied to material made from the hair of Angora goats, but these days the word often applies to fabric made of a wool and cotton blend. New mohair bears are expensive and often hard to find. To familiarize yourself with the material, you may have to learn on old bears. Again, an advanced collector or dealer might be willing to help. Although mohair can have either a soft or stiff feel to the touch, there is something distinctive and recognizable about it (its scent, for one thing).

Old Teddy Bears were stuffed with any of a variety of materials: straw (stiff and crackly, if you feel or squeeze a bear), excelsior (softer, pliable, sometimes crackly), kapok (softer, more huggable), wood-wool (firm). Kapok was also used for stuffing mattresses. It comes from the seed pods of trees that are sometimes referred to as silk-cotton trees. Wood-wool was a type of wood fiber that was processed to resemble wool. Some fine old bears have been filled with sawdust or even cork stuffing; others have cotton insides.

Before you go bear hunting, study pictures: old and new photographs, old prints, children's book illustrations, old magazine covers and illustrations. (Jessie Wilcox Smith and Bessie Pease Gutmann were two artists who used Teddy Bears as subjects.) This way, you'll be able to recognize the real thing when you see it.

When bear hunters search for related items, plates like this one are what they seek out.

Often a well-loved, and by now collectible, Teddy Bear has needed emergency repairs during its lifetime. Replacement paws will not greatly alter the value of an old bear, if they are a close match in color and texture, and if they are neatly done.

Replacement eyes are common and do not alter the value at all, if the replacements are still genuine old eyes. Shoe button and stickpin eyes often fell out or were removed by wise parents for safety reasons. These items can still be found in shops and at flea markets. They are good to buy and put away in case you need a set of authentic eyes at a later date. Plastic buttons and eyes should not be used on antique bears. They give a grotesque appearance to the Teddy.

If an arm or leg has been replaced, the Teddy is not considered to be in "mint" condition (close to perfect), especially if the part has been made of new fabric. The value, therefore, is less. How much less is entirely up to the purchaser, who should keep the replacement part in mind. At least a third off the standard value seems fair.

Examine your find

Clothes don't necessarily make the bear

If the bear being sold is wearing clothes, have the seller remove them before you buy. Clothes sometimes conceal a major flaw. We bought a bear that was wearing a white dress; one arm appeared to be longer than the other, but the dealer assured us it was our imagination. When we got home and removed the garment, not only were the arms unmatched, but the paws themselves were different shapes and sizes. Take advantage of our mistake.

By the way, if a bear is dressed up, be aware that the clothes may have been added by other than the original manufacturer; judge the price accordingly. You can always find clothes later, so don't be afraid to buy a bare bear.

This jointed old mohair fellow is splendidly dressed in a handmade plush coat with brass buttons, and a cap with a visor made from an old leather wallet. He carries a parasol made from a dress belonging to the owner's great grandmother. This is surely Teddy Bear haute couture.

The better antiques, for the most part, are jointed at the shoulders and have swivel heads. Remember though: man-made fibers and plastic eyes and noses are all part of the modern world. Don't let anyone sell you a bear with a plastic nose or nylon plush and represent it as seventy years old.

Internal squeakers, growlers and musical mechanisms may have been removed or put out of commission through the years. Sellers will tell you that this doesn't alter the value of the bear, and if everything else fills the bill—the bear is in good condition—you will probably pay about the same price as you would if the mechanism were working.

Beware of special toys like wind-ups, bellows music boxes, mechanicals, and any other perishable bears. Once the gadgetry stops working in these, you're in trouble—especially if you paid a high price because the toy was in working condition. Don't buy this kind of toy unless it's something that really appeals to you. You would be taking a risk.

Look out for reproductions and fakes when searching for antique bears. For example, there is a small jointed bear, originally made in Poland and distributed in the 1970s as a cute novelty, that has shown up at antique shows minus its label and with its plush dusty, and looking aged. At five or ten dollars the bear is still a cute novelty, but some antique dealers display it with a price of twenty-five dollars or more.

A quick word about prices

The guidelines in the price guide section of this book are suggestions. If you wish to study prices on your own, it is important to read three or four national publications to see how the market is going. The directory section has a listing of a few newspaper and magazine titles.

Go to at least three (and preferably more) antique shows. Be at the head of the line before the show opens. If good bears are for sale, they are frequently sold in the first few minutes after the opening. Therefore, the early bird gets a

chance to take a look before they're gone. Do the same thing at no fewer than three large flea markets in different locations. Price bears in at least two reputable antique shops.

Friendly dealers have told us that when checking a garage or house sale ad, you should avoid going to those advertised as multi-family sales. If more than one or two families hold a sale together, you can be reasonably sure one of those insiders will buy any really good bears before the sale ever opens, making your visit a waste of time.

All this might seem like a lot of additional work, but in the long run it will save you aggravation and disappointment. When all is said and done, lots of people still make mistakes. One experienced antique collector bought an expensive Steiff Teddy which was supposedly over a hundred years old. At the time of purchase, she had forgotten there were no Teddy Bears before 1902.

Opposite page: You-must-have-been-a-beautiful-baby Bear looks comfortable in this buggy. Often you can find old carriages at flea markets.

Speaking of Steiff

Be sure you know your Steiff products before you buy a Steiff antique. The company is considered by many to manufacture the Rolls Royces of Teddy Bears, so a Steiff bear is something you will want to learn how to identify. The company's main identifying trademark is a small silver-colored metal button with the name Steiff impressed into the metal. The button is inserted into the left ear of the bear by the company. Occasionally buttons appear at antique shows in the ears of bears which are not Steiff products, so there is always some risk involved. As you become more familiar with the antique bears, the risk will lessen.

One important note: some of those early buttons (1907 and earlier) were blank, they did not have "Steiff" on the surface. The buttons are firmly imbedded in the toys' left ears, and the bears are Steiff. Not many of these blank buttons appear to have survived; they are considered valuable.

Bear Care and Repair

Whether you own a collection of the most expensive antique bears or just a few that are brand new with future collectible potential, it is important to keep them in good condition.

A Teddy can still be a working bear—a toy that is played with, a mascot sitting on a bed or shelf, a traveling companion or a rearview mirror gymnast. Bear care does not require retirement from these duties.

New bears If a new bear is stored in a closed cabinet, it remains relatively maintenance-free. Just vacuum it lightly every few months with a lightweight portable vacuum cleaner (avoid heavy-duty power vacuums). If, however, it's stored where it gathers more dust, vacuum more frequently.

A bear that is frequently played with as a child's toy will need periodic baths. When the bear is tagged with its own cleaning instructions, follow them. Snip off the tag and save it in a safe, handy place. As a matter of fact, if you have a new bear you really like and want to save, take a photograph of it. Put the photo with any instruction tags (including the original price paid for the bear and the date purchased), and save all that material together. Should it ever become a collectible, everything can be put back in its original place, and you'll have additional background information as well.

Seam and rip repair Before bathing, go over the Teddy, checking for split seams or other minor damage. Poke the stuffing back in with the blunt end of a crochet hook. Find thread that matches the fabric as closely as possible, and sew the rip closed with small, close-together stitches, see page 39. Underarm and neck areas (especially around what would be the collarbones if Teddy Bears had them) usually show the strain first, so check there for damage.

Replacement eyes and tongues (red felt) can usually be found at quality craft stores: buy extra eyes and keep them in your "bear kit" so you'll have them when you need them. (When a child's favorite Teddy Bear is unexpectedly injured, it sometimes requires prompt skilled emergency surgery if you want to keep peace in the house.)

By writing the manufacturer and sending the bear model number from the tags you saved, you may sometimes get exact matches in replacement parts.

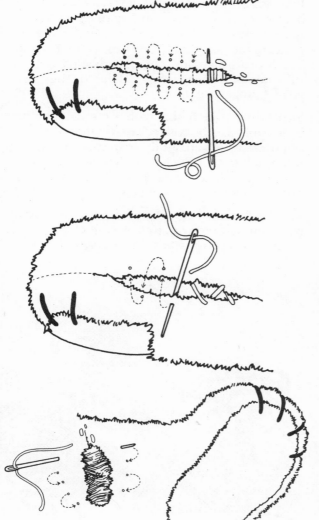

Ladder Stitch: Using thread that closely matches the color of the bear's fur, weave into and out of the fur as illustrated. Stay as close to the edge of the opening as possible making sure to poke in any leaking stuffing with the blunt end of a crochet hook.

Lacing Stitch: This, too, will hold the fur of the Teddy Bear firmly together. Follow the illustration being sure to enter the fur from the wrong side and to exit through the right side.

If the Teddy Bear is ripped, and the fur around the rip is very worn, use the ladder stitch, leaving as much as an inch of fur between the rip and the stitch. Tuck the worn fur under as you sew, easing it into the seam with the blunt end of a crochet hook.

Bathing your bear

Once you've given the bear a routine checkup, you can proceed with the bath. First, one caution that applies to all bears, old or new: what works for one person and bear might not work for others. There are differences in detergents, water, and touch. All caring and repairing instructions given here are suggestions that are based on what has worked best for us through the years. Anytime you work on a Teddy Bear, some risk is involved. If you do damage a bear, don't let it throw you. Try to figure out what went wrong, and develop a safer way to perform the task. An injured bear is still lovable. Teddy Bears may fade, sag, stain or shed, but their personalities are never affected. They just go on being perfect.

Meanwhile, back to that bath. First, vacuum the bear. Spots may be treated with laundry stain removers which are available in supermarkets. But be cautious. Check for colorfastness in an obscure spot like the back of a leg or the bear's bottom before proceeding elsewhere.

To shampoo the bear, place it on a table which has been covered with a clean terrycloth towel. Take a small pan of warm water and add

Teddy surrounded by some of the equipment needed to keep it in top shape. On the left: a self-standing blow dryer; basin; soft bristle brushes; metal dog comb.

approximately one-eighth capful of mild liquid detergent. Stir it to a sudsy froth with a fork. Use a new long-handled brush with soft bristles like those used to clean Teflon. Before brushing any liquid onto a bear, always lightly shake your brush in order to remove any excess and avoid waterlogging. Then, beginning with the head, brush on the suds, using overlapping clockwise light strokes. Keep cleaning the brush between applications by rinsing it in clear (preferably running) water and shaking it out.

After the bear has been lightly coated, take a clean washcloth, dip it in clear water, wring it out and damply (no soaking, please) wipe off the suds with light clockwise movements. As the cloth becomes soapy or soiled, use a new one or rinse the soapy one *thoroughly* before reapplying the cloth to the bear.

If you wish, you may add a second rinse by brushing on, with the same type of long-handled brush, a mixture of one-quarter capful fabric softener diluted in a bowl of clean warm water. Rinse the brush in clear water before dipping it into the bowl again.

Timesavers

By the way, there are three quick methods of applying cleaning solution to new bears. You can try a spray bottle like the ones used for plants. Put some of the detergent-and-water mixture in the bottle, shake well and adjust to fine spray. Lightly coat the bear, then gently scrub off the soap using a clean damp cloth and overlapping clockwise motions.

Some people use pump-bottles of bathroom cleaner as the initial detergent. If you want to try this method, you should check your bear for colorfastness and fabric strength first. Use an inconspicuous part of the bear for a testing spot.

The third method is a good cleaning shortcut even for old bears. After vacuuming, apply a color-safe carpet cleaner onto the fabric. Brush it lightly with a damp brush which you may have to moisten several times. Let it dry for twenty-four hours and then vacuum again.

Fresh air and sunshine No matter which method you choose, once the bear is rinsed, put it outside on a clean towel and let it dry in the sun if possible. Also, if you brush certain bears lightly while they are drying in outdoor breezes and sun, they fluff up. Try the softer side of a hand-and-nail brush.

One word of warning, new bear owners: some fabrics fade when left in the sun for too long. Don't plunk your bear in a sunny window and forget about it. A few hours of sun is plenty.

Some new bears may be machine-washed and/or dried in a clothes dryer. If you're using a dryer, put two or three dry bath towels in the machine, which should then be turned on for a few minutes before adding the bear. Always watch the drying time and temperature or you'll end up with a baked bear. Delicate fabric settings are usually the safest.

Once the bear is as good as new, clean all the equipment thoroughly and put it away in a box so you won't have to waste time regathering utensils the next time you're in the mood for bear washing.

Antique bears While some people leave venerable old bears in their darkened, matted condition, they look a lot better when they have been cleaned. Honest!

First, assemble the right equipment. Start with two small bowls, two long-handled, soft-bristle dishwashing brushes, two or three metal dog combs with variations in the set of the teeth, several terrycloth washcloths and towels, and at least one strong-powered hair dryer. We have found that two free-standing dog dryers (ours are made by Oster) work the best, because they blow the mohair fibers from different directions. This fluffs up the bear while freeing your hands to work with the comb.

When you first bring home a very old bear, check it carefully for insects. Do not take any chances. Some bears, stored for long periods in basements or attics, have yielded silverfish, moths, spiders, and a few other unwelcome parasites. It pays to be careful. Suspected bears

A bear, from the early 1900s, was a $5 house-sale purchase.

Antique jet beads were added for eyes; the body was restuffed, which also restored the hump in back and enabled the head to remain upright.

New arm, ears (velvet), and paws (felt) were added, plus a new suit ($5) and Teddy Roosevelt pin (an antique retrieved from the owner's jewelry box). Completed bear in this final condition might bring $100 or more.

should be placed in an appropriate isolation box, along with a new solid-stick insecticide. Most discount stores carry them. The box should be securely closed and left for forty-eight hours or so. This will result in the survival of the Teddy but the departure of any extra little guests.

Making do   Take a portable vacuum and carefully go over the bear. Check the seams as you go. If any are ripped, sew them with thread that matches as closely as possible (see page 39). In order to keep the bear as authentic as you can, use old thread you or your friends or relatives may have. If stuffing has leaked out, it must be replaced before you close the seams. Straw or excelsior can be found in old stuffed animals too far gone to save. They are easily obtained at garage and rummage sales at a very minimal expense (say fifty cents).

Remove the filler material from these and save it. At the same time, if they have glass stickpin eyes, retrieve them. These will come in handy when you find sightless bears who need fast, authentic transplants. Other stickpin eye donors may be stone-marten boas (you know, those little ferret-like things that sneer at you from flea market tables). These taxidermy eyes suit smaller antique bears very nicely.

If you are unable to find any of the correct materials, don't be discouraged. For stuffing you can cut up clean pantyhose or stockings (but discard the elastic bands) into very small scraps. This will fill sagging bear parts, and at the same time dry quickly after cleaning. Even if it is a modern replacement, it's a pleasure to work with such material—and it's a great use for torn unwearable stockings.

Pack the stuffing in *gently* with the blunt end of a crochet hook or the eraser end of a pencil— although the latter may be a little too thick. Unclog any internal packs of straw so you can intertwine the new filler with what's already inside. Never overstuff, because it puts too much strain on the aging fabric.

When you repair a rip in an old bear, sometimes the affected fabric is already frayed. You will have to discreetly stitch the fabric (from underneath) in areas as far away as an inch or so to make sure the repair will hold without further damaging the fabric (see page 39). If a ridge forms around the rip, gently push in the fabric ends so they don't show. By diverting the repair to a more stable area, you are spreading the stress and saving the bear from potential tragedy. Do nothing about missing or torn paw pads at this point.

This is the time to start the cleaning. Some owners use commercial dry cleaners on old bears and have been delighted with the outcome. The cleaners we interviewed, however, solemnly warn, "We will not guarantee anything, and this is done at your own risk." That's somber enough to scare us away. Besides, who wants to leave a Teddy Bear overnight in a dry cleaners without anyone around to reassure it or hold its paw?

This muff was renovated by removing a damaged doll's head and replacing it with a mohair Teddy Bear head: accomplished without damaging the swivel. A little creativity makes a really nice one-of-a-kind piece, probably now worth about $85.

Old bears need baths, too

We prefer cleaning antique bears at home. The process is similar to the washing instructions for new bears but it is slightly risky and should be done more slowly and delicately.

If the bear has stickpin eyes, remove them and stick them into a bar of soap. This will allow you to clean the mohair head thoroughly and the eyes will be easier to reinsert later.

After the bear has been thoroughly vacuumed, spread a large clean towel over a table and place the bear on it. Follow the instructions for bathing that appear on page 40. For some older bears, when we feel it is really needed, we also add a little liquid chlorine bleach to this mixture, with very good results. Don't try this until you're experienced, however, because of the risk.

Keep a second bowl filled with clear warm water. Once the head has been soaped, take the second brush and, using only clear water from the second bowl, repeat the process to rinse off the soapy residue. A clean, damp washcloth can also be used for this stage. Be careful not to disturb the nose-and-mouth stitching.

As a final step, rinse one more time by dipping the clean brush into a clean bowl of warm water to which ¼- to ½-capful of fabric softener (preferably the kind with bluing) has been added and thoroughly mixed. Brush this on (light circular strokes), further removing any soap from the fabric. Again, keep the brush clean between applications by running it through clear water and shaking off the excess. Remember, never let the bear get too wet, and keep in mind that when it's damp, if you hold the animal too firmly, you will shift the stuffing.

After the head has been completely washed, do the torso, then the limbs. Skip the paws, keeping them as dry as possible if they are felt or any other fabric that might be damaged by water. Also, avoid the digit stitching where the arms join the felt of the paws.

When the whole bear has been completed, place it on a thick towel. Turn on the dryer and, beginning with the head, carefully, gently, cautiously, insert the comb at the base of the matted mohair (or other fur fiber). Lift it, fluffing it with the dryer as you work in order to restore the pile. Never let a hot dryer get too close to the bear; take your time while you work.

Now repeat the whole process on the torso; after that do the limbs.

During this comb-and-dry process, be careful not to rip the fabric with the comb. Be sure the metal teeth are not too sharp. (You can dull them with a file or Moto-Tool, if you have to.) Vary the combs, starting with wider-spaced teeth if there is a great deal of pressed-down matting. Facial fur is especially well restored if it is finished off with a fine-tooth "flea" comb (available at pet shops).

When the entire bear has been combed, it will still be damp. Place it on a dry white towel outdoors, if possible, or suspend it from a clothesline using nylon fishing line (tied loosely around the waist not the neck). Warm sun and breezes, plus occasional fluff-up combing by you, will do the rest. Meanwhile, dip the glass part of the eyes in ammonia, then rinse, dry, and replace in the bear.

If it's winter, and you have heat registers, forced air heat will help complete the process. Fold a clean towel about ten inches from a register and seat the bear on that. From time to time, using the outdoor or indoor drying method, turn and refluff the animal.

Paw repair

As soon as it is dry, finish the bear by replacing any of the paw felt you feel is unsatisfactory. Search the usual antique haunts for old felt hats, coat or purse linings. If you can't find any authentic paw materials, buy new felt in as close a matching fabric as possible. See page 48 for illustrated instructions on replacing paw felt.

If you are an expert at needlework, you can devise other ways to do authentic-looking repair work. Half the fun and feeling of accomplishment in all this is the pleasure of discovery and innovation.

Using the shape illustrated, cut a piece of felt or other fabric ¼- to ½-inch larger on all sides than the size needed. One-quarter-to ½-inch in from the edge, make a dotted line around the fabric. Snip out tiny V-shapes from the edge of the fabric to the line, evenly spaced around the entire piece.

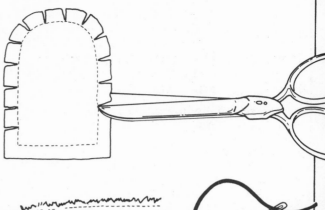

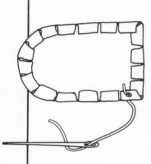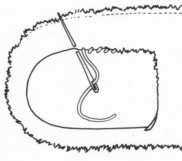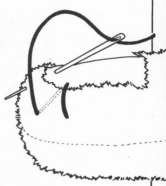

Iron under the snipped edge. Using matching thread strong enough to hold the felt to the bear's fur, make a knot in the thread end and sew into the paw. The knot should fall on the wrong side of the felt.

Place the paw fabric over the old paw fabric or where the old fabric originally was. Sew it down using tiny stitches, as illustrated. Bring some of the bear's fur up over the paw fabric to hide the stitches.

To make digits on the paw, use thick black upholstery thread and sew as illustrated. The knot on the thread should be hidden by the bear's fur. If not, gently push it beneath the fabric and into the stuffing.

Replacing a button eye

For example, if you need shoe button eyes and can't find any the right size and shape, color round beads with a black marking pen, then dip them in colorless nail polish. Beads from an old necklace often have metal loops which can be straightened with needlenose pliers to become stickpins—perfect for eyes.

Or if the bear is missing an eye, and you can't find a replacement, make an eye patch, and your bear will look swashbuckling. If it is missing a paw or an arm, make a plaster cast and tell folks the arm was broken in a skiing accident.

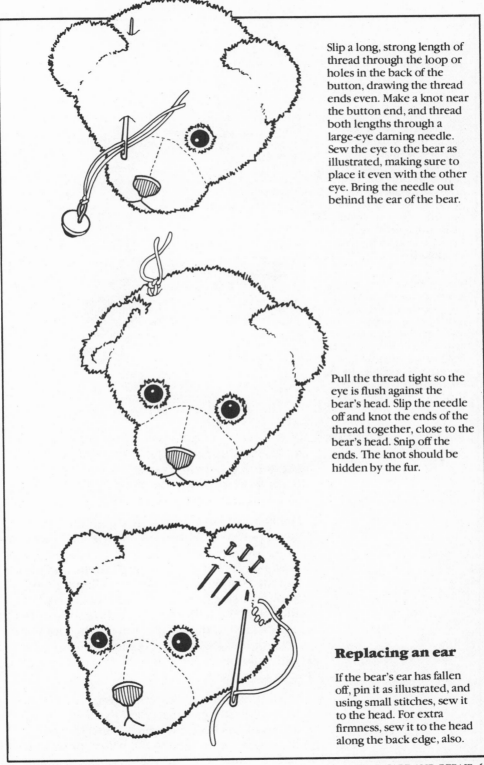

Slip a long, strong length of thread through the loop or holes in the back of the button, drawing the thread ends even. Make a knot near the button end, and thread both lengths through a large-eye darning needle. Sew the eye to the bear as illustrated, making sure to place it even with the other eye. Bring the needle out behind the ear of the bear.

Pull the thread tight so the eye is flush against the bear's head. Slip the needle off and knot the ends of the thread together, close to the bear's head. Snip off the ends. The knot should be hidden by the fur.

Replacing an ear

If the bear's ear has fallen off, pin it as illustrated, and using small stitches, sew it to the head. For extra firmness, sew it to the head along the back edge, also.

Nose and mouth repair

With light-weight thread, make a nose and mouth shape using small running stitches as illustrated by the dotted line. The size of the nose and mouth is determined by the size of the Teddy Bear. Fill in the shape with embroidery thread, using stitches that are close together.

Making one neat stitch across, finish off the top of the nose shape. Use one stitch apiece to make the line down from the nose and each side of the mouth. If any of the knots in the thread are not hidden by the fur, ease them under the stitches so they don't show.

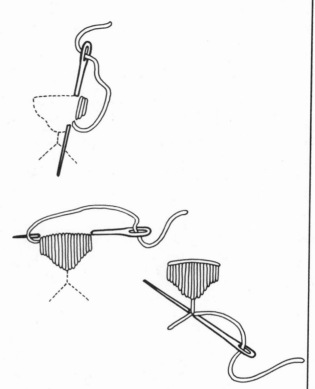

Calling in a doctor

We did a plaster cast repair with a veterinarian, Dr. Mark A. Rutman of Chesterland, Ohio. We liked the way it turned out and asked the good doctor to write down the "prescription" in case you needed the brand names.

"The bear is laid on its side with the affected limb uppermost. Stirrups of one-inch diameter medical adhesive tape (Zonas Porous Tape, Johnson & Johnson) are applied to the end of the limb to prevent the cast from slipping. An orthopedic stockinette (Abco Products) is pulled over the limb to prevent the cast material from sticking to the fur. To prevent the cast from being applied too tightly, cotton padding (Cast Padding, Johnson & Johnson) is wrapped around the stockinette.

"A large bowl of cool water is prepared. A roll of two-inch plaster cast material (Extra Fast Setting Plaster of Paris Cast, Two Inch Rolls, Johnson & Johnson) is submerged in the water for several seconds. The excess water is then squeezed from the material with some care being taken to prevent too much of the plaster material from falling off into the bowl.

"The application of the cast is begun at the lower end of the limb and encircles it with each layer overlapping the previous layer by fifty percent. If needed, a second layer of cast material is applied over the first in a similar manner. The bear should be kept immobilized until the cast has dried completely, usually about fifteen minutes."

A cast can be used permanently or as a temporary aid until you can make the correct repair.

When we brought this bear home it was missing a paw and leaking stuffing from its wound. We had a veterinarian show us how to apply a real cast and were so pleased with the result that we almost kept it on for good. Eventually we rebuilt the missing paw and fixed the leak.

Teddy Bear Price Guide

French Mechanical
8 inches;
1880; French; clockwork
"Martin"; wind-up; very rare
$1,000

Pricing bears

This section has been put together to show you approximate contemporary market prices of old, or discontinued modern, collectible bears. We have attempted to include bears in all price ranges, so that beginning collectors can try their luck knowing what to look for in their price range, while advanced collectors, more willing to spend greater amounts of money, can better identify of real treasures and know their approximate monetary value.

Prices were carefully researched for years over a geographically large area by a study of antique shows, auctions, flea markets, individual collectors, manufacturers, and printed advertising prices in newspapers and magazines. Keep in mind that prices on individual bears depend upon age, rarity (Were there only a few made?), appeal (Is it irresistible?), quality, uniqueness (Was it a commemorative issue; a special occasion design; a specific character; a different sort of mechanical?), and the general market for that particular bear.

In the text related to the photographs, all clothes were added after the bear left the manufacturer or retailer, unless you see the phrase "original clothes."

Also keep in mind: stuffings vary. Sometimes even very early owners changed stuffing when washing or repairing old bears. In addition, more than one type of stuffing was used in some bears. A bear stuffed with straw, for instance, may have had a kapok or wood-wool torso. During our years of snooping around (and into) bears, we've run into all sorts of stuffings: cotton, rag filler, tiny cork pieces, strips of rolled paper, sawdust, shredded foam rubber, wool, straw, excelsior, and all sorts of man-made materials. The stuffing mentioned with specific photographs is the primary material used in that particular bear.

Because so many collectors think of old bears as being straw stuffed, and have referred to them as such for so many years, bears that feel crackly to the touch will be referred to in this price guide

Be sure to dress your Teddy Bears in suitable clothing. This flea market find told us she was really Scarlett O'Hara so we dressed her in an outfit that would win the heart of any Rhett Butler.

as straw stuffed. You may wish to keep in mind that the crackly feel may mean the bear is not stuffed with straw but with excelsior. (Straw usually refers to dry stems or stalks of grain, while excelsior is made of long thin wood shavings.) The price value of straw- or excelsior-filled bears should be the same.

This price guide is to be used as a reference as well as a guideline. The prices listed are, unless otherwise designated, for bears in mint (or near-mint) condition. That means that if you're trying to sell a bear exactly like one pictured in this section, but if yours has worn, soiled, or damaged fur—your asking price should be lowered accordingly. The same rule applies to disfigured heads, loose limbs, destroyed paws, broken mechanisms, and any other damages the bear may have incurred. Keep this in mind if you are buying a bear as well. If it is overpriced and very damaged, look for a better buy.

The height in inches listed with each bear, if not exact, is a close approximation. Bears of the same design may not always measure the same length, due to differences in the amount of stuffing in each. Also, fabric pile often fluctuates: a balded old bear we measure will be slightly shorter than the one you've found of the same design which still has all its fur.

One word about eyes, too. As we have stated previously, many were removed for safety reasons during the owner's childhood. Replacements, if they are genuinely old, should not detract from a bear's value. Acceptable replacements are old shoe buttons (the flat-back type fit the head better than the rounded-back) and glass stickpin eyes.

Genuinely old handmade clothes, obviously custom-sewn for the bear wearing them, also are a value plus to many buyers. A bear with its own period wardrobe would command a higher price, even if those clothes were made after the bear was purchased.

Meanwhile, lots of good luck and happy bear hunting!

Large Mechanical Bear

25 inches;
fur over papier mâché body; carved head; glass eyes; mechanism makes head move up and down.
$850

Little Dressed Cub

Sitting Bear

Teddy Bears

Little Dressed Cub
2½ inches;
1970s; Shackman;
plush; jointed limbs;
swivel head.
$5

Sitting Bear
3 inches;
circa 1930s; brown
plush over wood; glass
eyes; black stickpin
metal nose; stiff body.
$18

Little Gold Bear
3 inches;
gold velvet; glass eyes;
jointed limbs; very
high shoulders.
$35

Little Gold Bear

Bear Trio

Nutshell Bear

Baby Bear

Bear Trio
3½ inches to
5½ inches;
early 1900s; Steiff;
white mohair; shoe
button eyes; jointed
limbs; swivel heads;
humps.
$85 each

Nutshell Bear
3½ inches;
German; Schuco; tan
mohair; black, sewn
nose and mouth;
jointed limbs; swivel
head.
Molded Nutshell:
German; paper;
added later.
Nutshell: $10
Bear: $45

Baby Bear
3½ inches;
early 1900s; Steiff;
mohair; straw stuffed;
shoe button eyes;
black, sewn nose and
mouth; jointed limbs;
swivel head.
$85

Long-nose Bear

Two-faced Bear, both faces

Bear Pals

Long-nose Bear
3½ inches;
1950s; German; brown
mohair; paper and
cotton stuffed; brown,
sewn nose and mouth;
jointed limbs.
$15

Two-faced Bear
3½ inches;
circa 1950; German;
Schuco; brown plush;
black button-type eyes;
black, sewn nose and
mouth; jointed limbs;
screw at bottom turns
head to reveal second
face.
$55

Bear Pals
3½ inches and
5½ inches;
Steiff; gold mohair;
straw stuffed; black,
sewn noses and
mouths; jointed limbs;
swivel heads.
3½ inches: $65
5½ inches: $85

Busy Bear

High-shouldered Bear

Busy Bear
4 inches;
Japanese; straw stuffed;
tiny glass stickpin
eyes; black, metal nose;
loosely jointed.
Tin Telephone: $5
Bear: $25

High-shouldered Bear
4 inches;
brown velvet; glass
eyes; jointed at hips
and shoulders.
$35

Frowning Bear
4½ inches;
1940s; gold mohair;
glass stickpin eyes;
jointed limbs.
$40

Wide-eyed Bear
5 inches;
circa 1940s; yellow
plush; wood-wool-like
stuffing; glass stickpin
eyes; black, sewn nose
and mouth; jointed
limbs; chubby body.
$35

Frowning Bear

Wide-eyed Bear

Animal Trainer

Chubby Polar Bear

Fuzzy Bear

Animal Trainer
5½ inches; circa 1910; Steiff; gold mohair; shoe button eyes; black sewn nose and mouth; jointed limbs; swivel head; hump.
Pull-toy Donkey: gray felt; shoe button eyes; old metal bell; red felt saddle; leather harness; wood wheels; head bobs up and down as it rolls.
Donkey: $55
Bear: $85

Chubby Polar Bear
5½ inches; white mohair; plush muzzle; soft stuffed; glass eyes; black, sewn nose and mouth; jointed limbs.
Handmade Rug: new; needlepoint.
Rug: $35
Bear: $40

Fuzzy Bear
6 inches; English; brown and cream, wool-type plush; soft stuffed; black button eyes; black, sewn nose and mouth.
Wood Bear: German; jointed limbs; movable head.
Wood: $3
Fuzzy: $30

Bedtime Bears

Swiss Miss

Steiff's "Jackie"

Bedtime Bears

6 inches;
early 1900s; Steiff;
brown mohair; straw
stuffed; glass eyes;
brown, sewn noses
and mouths; jointed
limbs; swivel heads;
original ribbons.
Wooden Bed: maple.
Bed: $15
Bears: $85 each

Swiss Miss

6 inches;
Swiss; Felpa; brown
mohair; black, sewn
nose and mouth;
cream muzzle and
paws; bendable;
original skirt and bow;
"Mutzli" on tag.
$35

Steiff's "Jackie"

6½ inches;
1953; mohair; brown,
sewn nose (with single
white stitch) and
mouth; felt paws;
jointed limbs; swivel
head; squeaker;
elongated muzzle;
original red ribbon
around neck; "Jubilee
Teddy" on original tag;
U.S. zone-Germany on
label under right arm.
Jackie was the 50-year
Steiff commemorative
bear (1903-1953)
$175 and up

Dakin's "Misha"

Toe-touching Bear

Scooter Bear

Dakin's "Misha"

7 inches;
1980; "Misha-Official Mascot of 1980 Moscow Olympic Games" on tag; must have original Olympic belt; larger sizes available.
$15 and up

Toe-touching Bear

7 inches;
early 1900s; gold mohair; straw stuffed; shoe button eyes; black, sewn nose and mouth; jointed limbs; swivel head with long, upturned nose; squeaker; hump; elongated torso and limbs; unusual.
$85-$100

Scooter Bear

7 inches (including wheels);
plush; "U.S. zone-Germany" on metal scooter; wind-up mechanism.
In working condition: $100

Little-bodied Bear

Wind-up Walker

Little-bodied Bear

8 inches;
early 1900s; mohair;
glass eyes; brown,
sewn, elongated
muzzle; felt paws;
jointed limbs; swivel
head; squeaker; hump;
very appealing.
$110

Wind-up Walker

8 inches;
1920s; German;
Gebrüder-Bing;
mohair; shoe button
eyes; black, sewn nose
and mouth; felt paws;
wooden walking stick;
original yellow felt
jacket and blue cotton
pants.
$300

Schuco's "Rolly"

8½ inches;
German; brown
mohair; roller skating
wind-up; "Made in
U.S. Zone-Germany"
on tag.
$250

Schuco's "Rolly"

Ballerina Bear

Circus Bear

Big Bow Bear

Ballerina Bear
9 inches;
early 1900s; mohair;
straw stuffed; glass
eyes; brown, sewn
nose and mouth; felt
paws; jointed limbs;
swivel head.
$125

Circus Bear
9 inches;
early 1900s; Steiff; gold
mohair; straw stuffed;
glass eyes; black, sewn
nose and mouth; felt
paws; jointed limbs;
swivel head; hump;
original clown hat and
ruffled collar.
$175

Big Bow Bear
9 inches;
1907; Steiff; gold
mohair; straw stuffed;
shoe button eyes;
black, sewn nose and
mouth; felt paws;
jointed limbs; swivel
head; squeaker; hump;
finest quality.
$165 and up

Tumbling Bear, two positions

Long-limbed Puppet Bear

Tumbling Bear
9½ inches;
1920s; German;
Gebrüder-Bing;
original green felt
jacket and yellow
pants; wind-up arms
enable bear to
somersault; "BW"
on metal arm tag.
$300

Long-limbed Puppet Bear
9½ inches;
mohair; shoe button
eyes; jointed limbs; tail
operates head
movement.
$185 and up

Cocoa Bear
10 inches;
1940s; Character;
brown plush; soft
stuffed; black button-
type eyes fastened over
white felt.
$25

Cocoa Bear

Simple Bear

Simple Bear

10 inches;
1940s; Japanese; gold
mohair; straw stuffed;
glass eyes; black, sewn
nose and mouth;
jointed limbs move as
pairs, no separate
movement.
$55

Sunday Driver Bears

10 inches and 8 inches;
1960s; German; gold
mohair; glass-type
eyes; felt paws; jointed
limbs; swivel heads;
squeakers.
8 inches: $55
10 inches: $65

Sunday Driver Bears

Roller Skater

Pulling Bear

Riding Bear

Roller Skater
11 inches;
1930s; long-haired
mohair; soft stuffed;
glass stickpin eyes;
black, sewn nose and
mouth; jointed limbs
(clothes and skates not
original).
$65

Pulling Bear
10½ inches;
brown mohair; slightly
cross-eyed; open
mouth; felt paws;
jointed limbs; swivel
head; very cute.

Riding Bear
11 inches;
plush; soft stuffed;
blue and white
checked body; metal
tricycle with red
wooden wheels; legs
pedal as trike is pulled.
Pulling: $110
Riding: $85

Bellhop Bear

Door-stop Bear

Long-haired Pair

Bellhop Bear
11 inches;
mohair; straw stuffed;
shoe button eyes;
black, sewn nose and
mouth; felt paws;
jointed limbs; swivel
head; red felt jacket
and hat; very large feet;
tail movement
controls head; rare.
$250 and up

Door-stop Bear
11 inches;
circa 1940s; dark
brown mohair; tan
mohair ears and
muzzle; glass stickpin
eyes; black, molded
nose; black, sewn
mouth; swivel head;
short stubby tail;
weighted body.
$65

Long-haired Pair
11 inches and 15
inches;
circa 1930s; long, pale
yellow-gold mohair;
soft stuffed; glass stickpin eyes; black, sewn
nose and mouth; felt
paws; jointed limbs;
swivel heads.
11 inches: $65
15 inches: $85

Pink Bear

Tough-guy Bear

Googlie-eyed Bear

Pink Bear
11½ inches;
circa 1920s; rare pink
mohair; soft stuffed;
glass eyes; black, sewn
nose and mouth; fabric
paws; jointed limbs;
swivel head.
$175

Tough-guy Bear
12 inches;
1930s; gold mohair;
straw stuffed; glass
eyes; black, sewn nose
and mouth; felt paws;
jointed limbs; swivel
head; pouty face.
$110

Googlie-eyed Bear
12 inches;
1970s; German;
Heinhauser; plush;
black, sewn nose;
painted mouth; jointed
limbs; squeaker.
$15

Perky Bear

Lazy Bear

Big-eared Bear

Hockey Player

Perky Bear
12 inches;
early 1900s; Ideal;
mohair; straw and
excelsior stuffed; shoe
button eyes; black,
sewn nose and mouth;
large felt paws; jointed
limbs; swivel head;
distinctive face and
expression; very rare.
$300 and up

Lazy Bear
12 inches;
early 1900s; mohair;
straw stuffed; shoe
button eyes; black,
sewn nose and mouth;
felt paws; jointed
limbs; swivel head;
hump.
Bottle: 1920s; blown
glass; individual
"honey server."
Bottle: $5
Bear: $185

Big-eared Bear
12 inches;
early 1900s; tan
mohair; straw stuffed;
shoe button eyes;
black, sewn nose and
mouth; felt paws;
jointed limbs; swivel
head; hump.
Chair: 1920s;
salesman's sample.
Chair: $75 and up
Bear: $175

Hockey Player
12 inches;
1970s; Steiff; soft
stuffed; felt open
mouth; original hockey
stick and very realistic
skates; hard to find;
extremely collectible.
$150 and up

Figure Skater

Merrythought's "Cheeky"

Figure Skater
12 inches; early 1900s; gold mohair; straw stuffed; glass stickpin eyes; black, sewn nose and mouth; felt paws; jointed limbs; swivel head; squeaker; hump. $125

Merrythought's "Cheeky"
12 inches; English; light brown plush; jointed limbs; swivel head; unusual face; label on right foot; very well made. $65

Hi, There Bear
12 inches; Steiff; gold mohair; straw stuffed; glass eyes; brown, sewn nose and mouth; felt paws; jointed limbs; swivel head; squeaker (stand not original). $110

Hi, There Bear

Dressed Country Bears

Dressed Country Bears

12 inches; modern; Steiff; soft stuffed; original clothes; sold exclusively by F.A.O. Schwarz, New York.
Each: $150 and up

Bon Vivants

12 inches; early 1900s; Steiff; mohair; straw stuffed; shoe button eyes; black, sewn noses and mouths; felt paws; jointed limbs; swivel heads; squeakers; humps.
Each: $185 and up

Bon Vivants

Casual Bear

Quizzical Bear

Worn-patch Bear

Casual Bear

13 inches; early 1900s; Steiff; mohair; straw stuffed; shoe button eyes; felt paws; jointed limbs; swivel head; hump. $185 and up

Quizzical Bear

13 inches; early 1900s; soft brown mohair; straw stuffed; glass eyes; elongated muzzle with black, sewn nose, and mouth; felt paws; wide-set ears; jointed limbs; swivel head; squeaker; hump; very nice, unusual expression. $165 and up

Worn-patch Bear

13 inches; early 1900s; Steiff; gold mohair; straw stuffed; shoe button eyes; black, sewn nose and mouth; felt paws; jointed limbs; swivel head; growler; hump; worn spots on body. $125 and up

Ice Skaters

Short-hair Bear

Serious Bear

Ice Skaters
13 inches;
early 1900s; gold
mohair; straw stuffed;
glass stickpin eyes;
black, sewn noses and
mouths; felt paws;
jointed limbs; swivel
heads; squeakers;
skates and clothes not
original.
$125 each

Short-hair Bear
13 inches;
gold plush; soft stuffed;
black button eyes;
black, sewn nose and
mouth; velvet paws;
jointed limbs; round,
swivel head; elongated
muzzle.
$55

Serious Bear
13 inches;
circa 1920s; brown
mohair; straw stuffed;
glass eyes; brown,
sewn nose and mouth;
felt paws; jointed
limbs; swivel head;
squeaker; small hump;
very appealing.
$100 and up

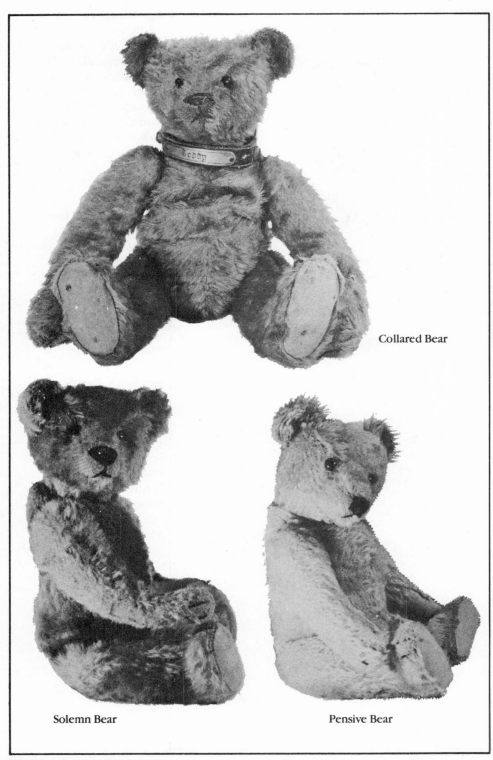

Collared Bear

Solemn Bear

Pensive Bear

Attentive Bear

Collared Bear
13 inches;
early 1900s; Steiff;
brown mohair; straw
stuffed; jointed limbs;
old collar with
engraved "Teddy" tag,
not original.
$165 and up

Solemn Bear
13 inches;
early 1900s; Steiff; gold
mohair; straw stuffed;
shoe button eyes;
black, sewn nose and
mouth; felt paws;
jointed limbs; swivel
head; squeaker; hump.
$185 and up

Pensive Bear
13 inches;
1920s; light brown
mohair; straw stuffed;
glass eyes; black, sewn
nose and mouth; felt
paws; jointed limbs;
swivel head; squeaker;
small hump.
$100 and up

Attentive Bear
13 inches;
Steiff; straw stuffed;
glass eyes; black, sewn
nose and mouth; felt
paws; jointed limbs;
swivel head; hump.
$150

Stand-up Comedian

Rolling-eye Bear

Over-stuffed Bear

Stand-up Comedian
13 inches;
brown plush head;
cloth-covered body;
glass stickpin eyes;
hard-soled, sewn-on
shoes; unusual.
$10

Rolling-eye Bear
13 inches;
late 1940s/early 1950s;
brown plush; soft
stuffed; plastic eyes;
black, sewn nose and
mouth; felt paws; high-
set ears; jointed limbs;
swivel head.
$35

Over-stuffed Bear
13 inches;
1940s; dark brown
mohair; soft stuffed;
glass stickpin eyes; felt
muzzle with black,
sewn nose and mouth;
felt upper paws;
cuddly appearance.
$55

Bat-eared Bear

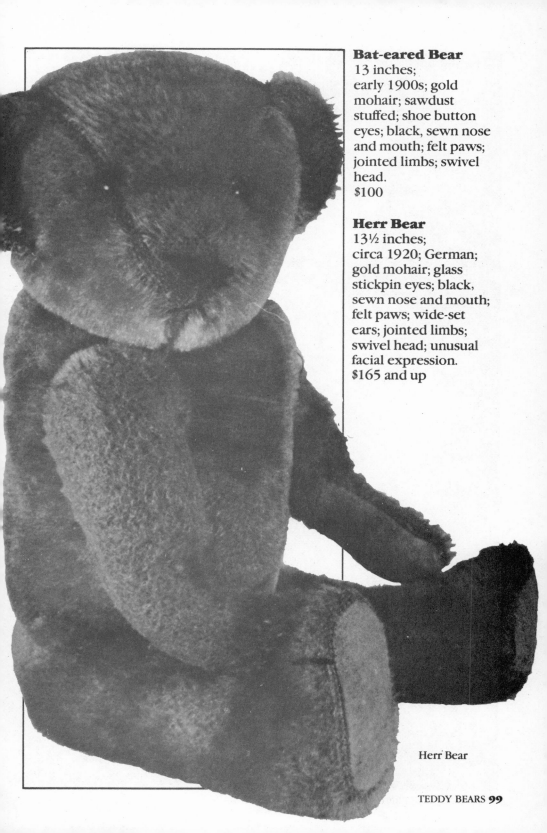

Bat-eared Bear
13 inches;
early 1900s; gold
mohair; sawdust
stuffed; shoe button
eyes; black, sewn nose
and mouth; felt paws;
jointed limbs; swivel
head.
$100

Herr Bear
13½ inches;
circa 1920; German;
gold mohair; glass
stickpin eyes; black,
sewn nose and mouth;
felt paws; wide-set
ears; jointed limbs;
swivel head; unusual
facial expression.
$165 and up

Herr Bear

Shaggy Bear

Farmer Bear

Wide-hipped
Bear

Shaggy Bear
13½ inches;
circa 1930s; long
white mohair;
straw stuffed;
glass eyes; black, sewn
nose and mouth; felt
paws; jointed limbs;
swivel head; squeaker.
$140

Farmer Bear
13½ inches;
gold mohair; straw
stuffed; glass eyes;
black, sewn nose and
mouth; felt paws;
jointed limbs; swivel
head; squeaker; very
hard to the touch.
$100

Wide-hipped Bear
13½ inches;
dark brown plush;
solidly stuffed;
elongated muzzle with
black, sewn nose and
mouth; felt paws;
jointed limbs.
$55

Wool Bear

Straight-back Bear

Funny-faced Bear

Wool Bear
14 inches;
early 1900s; brown
wool fabric; straw
stuffed; shoe button
eyes; black, sewn nose
and mouth; felt paws;
jointed limbs; swivel
head.
$135

Straight-back Bear
14 inches;
1930s; plush; straw
stuffed; glass eyes;
black, sewn nose and
mouth; red felt paws;
jointed limbs; swivel
head; squeaker; hump;
elongated body with
short arms.
$65

Funny-faced Bear
14 inches;
1920s; gold mohair;
straw stuffed; glass
stickpin eyes; black,
sewn nose and mouth;
felt paws; jointed
limbs; swivel head.
Little Cottage: old
wooden string-holder
with lift-off top.
Cottage: $25
Bear: $120

Rare Bear Pair

Rare Bear Pair
15 inches; early 1900s; Steiff; white mohair; soft stuffed; shoe button eyes; light brown sewn noses and mouths; felt paws; jointed limbs; swivel heads; squeakers; humps; rare pair; more valuable as a matched set.
$350 each

Steiff's "Cosy Teddy"
15 inches; 1970s; white plush with brown under neck; soft stuffed; glass-like eyes; brown, sewn nose; open felt mouth; felt paws.
$150

Steiff's "Cosy Teddy"

Steiff's "Minky Zotty"

Surprised Bear

Small-eared Bear

Steiff's "Minky Zotty"

15 inches;
1970s; platinum-mink-colored plush; brown, sewn nose; felt open mouth; growler; luxurious texture and appearance.
Tin Box: squeaking wooden clown pops out when button at bottom is pulled.
Box: $55
Bear: $150 and up

Surprised Bear

15 inches;
1930s; brown mohair; soft stuffed; glass stickpin eyes; black, sewn nose and mouth; felt paws; jointed limbs; swivel head.
Old Wind-up Birds: German; plush-covered metal bodies.
Bird Pair: $35 and up
Bear: $95

Small-eared Bear

15 inches;
early 1900s; white mohair; straw stuffed; glass stickpin eyes; light brown, sewn nose and mouth; linen paws; jointed limbs; swivel head; thin limbs.
$125

Yellow Fellow

Semi-ferocious Bear

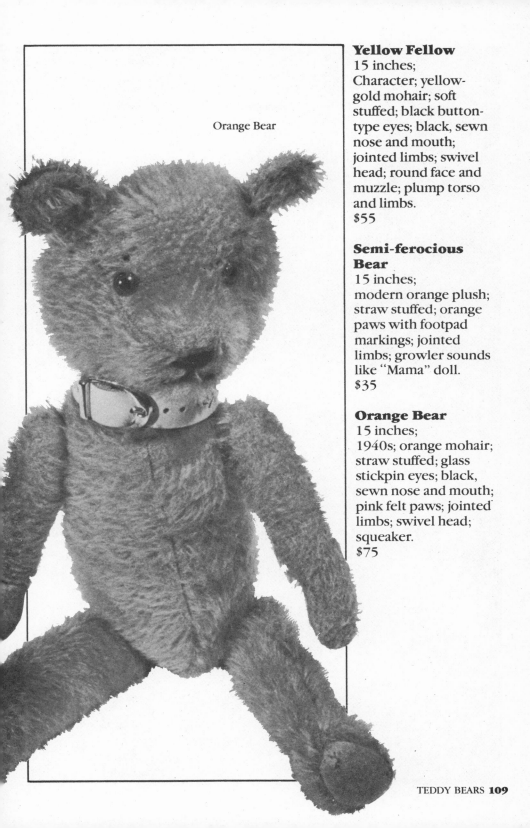

Orange Bear

Yellow Fellow
15 inches;
Character; yellow-gold mohair; soft stuffed; black button-type eyes; black, sewn nose and mouth; jointed limbs; swivel head; round face and muzzle; plump torso and limbs.
$55

Semi-ferocious Bear
15 inches;
modern orange plush; straw stuffed; orange paws with footpad markings; jointed limbs; growler sounds like "Mama" doll.
$35

Orange Bear
15 inches;
1940s; orange mohair; straw stuffed; glass stickpin eyes; black, sewn nose and mouth; pink felt paws; jointed limbs; swivel head; squeaker.
$75

Musical Maestro

Irresistible Bear

Sweet-looking Bear

Musical Maestro
15 inches;
circa 1930s; long
white mohair; glass
eyes; black, sewn nose
and mouth; felt paws;
jointed limbs; swivel
head; music box in
torso activated by
squeezing; unusual.
$175

Irresistible Bear
15 inches;
1910-1920; straw
stuffed; shoe button
eyes; black, sewn nose
and mouth; felt paws;
jointed limbs; swivel
head; squeaker; hump.
$150

Sweet-looking
Bear
15 inches;
early 1900s; gold
mohair; straw and
kapok stuffed; shoe
button eyes; black,
sewn nose and mouth;
hard-soled feet; very
wide-set ears; jointed
limbs; swivel head;
squeaker; hump.
$150 and up

Dancing Bear Pair

Staring Bear

Englishbear

Dancing Bear Pair
15 inches;
and 12 inches;
circa 1910; Steiff; glass eyes; sewn noses and mouths; jointed limbs; swivel heads; male bear dressed in blue jacket and blue plaid pants; female bear's dress has blue skirt and violet bodice (original clothes); bears are attached at paws and shoulders; rare.
Pair: $750

Staring Bear
15 inches;
1930s; gold mohair; straw stuffed; glass stickpin eyes; black, sewn nose and mouth; jointed limbs; swivel head; hump; thin torso and limbs.
$125

Englishbear
15 inches;
1950s; English; Chad Valley; gold mohair; soft stuffed; black, sewn nose and mouth; brown felt paws; jointed limbs; swivel head.
$65 and up

Ideal's Collector's Edition

Minstrel Bear

Studious Bear

Jerome

Ideal's Collector's Edition
16 inches;
1978; 75th anniversary commemorative; brown plush; lighter muzzle and paws; excellent quality; "The Original Ideal Teddy Bear" on tag; special edition box.
$20

Minstrel Bear
16 inches;
circa 1950s; brown curly poodle-cloth head and paws; soft stuffed; glass eyes; brightly colored, stitched-on-clothing-covered body; satin-like foot pads and ear linings.
$10

Studious Bear
16 inches;
circa 1930s; long, wavy yellow-gold mohair; soft stuffed; glass eyes; black, sewn nose and mouth; felt paws; jointed limbs; swivel head.
Walt Disney book: 1930s.
Bear only: $80

Jerome
16 inches;
early 1900s; mohair; soft stuffed; shoe button eyes; wearing vintage clothing; named by current owner; rare.
$200 and up

Growling Bear

Growling Bear
16 inches;
1920s; brown or green
mohair; straw stuffed;
glass stickpin eyes;
black, sewn nose and
mouth; fabric paws;
jointed limbs; swivel
head; wire handle
cranks internal tin
grinder to make faint
growling noise.
In working condition:
$120

Round-faced Bear
16 inches;
light gold mohair;
wood-wool stuffed;
shoe button eyes;
black, sewn nose and
mouth; felt paws;
jointed limbs; swivel
head; squeaker; hump;
elongated torso; short
legs.
$150

Round-faced Bear

Jester Bear

Jester Bear
16 inches;
early 1900s; German;
green mohair body;
straw stuffed; shoe
button eyes; elongated
nose; swivel head; very
long arms; original felt
clown collar and cuffs.
$350

Shaggy Bear
17 inches;
1920s; Steiff; gold
mohair; straw stuffed;
glass eyes; brown,
sewn nose and mouth;
felt paws; jointed
limbs; swivel head.
$185 and up

Steiff's "Zotty"
17 inches;
brown-and-cream
shaded fur; brown,
sewn nose; open felt
mouth; felt paws;
jointed limbs; swivel
head; growler.
$150

Shaggy Bear

Steiff's "Zotty"

Bulky Bear

Santa Bear

Smiling Bear

Bulky Bear
17 inches;
early 1900s; cotton
fabric; straw stuffed;
shoe button eyes;
original clothes;
unusual.
$150 and up

Santa Bear
17 inches;
white mohair; soft
stuffed; glass stickpin
eyes; jointed arms;
floppy legs; swivel
head; wind-up music
box plays "Jingle
Bells"; replaced Santa
Claus suit.
$95

Smiling Bear
17 inches;
1950s; Ideal; brown
plush; soft stuffed;
plastic eyes; molded
nose and mouth;
cream plush paws;
squeaker in tail.
$40

Plain Bear

Plain Bear
18 inches;
1912; gold mohair;
straw stuffed; shoe
button eyes; black,
sewn nose and mouth;
jointed limbs; swivel
head.
$110

Leaning Bear
18 inches;
gold mohair; straw
stuffed; glass eyes;
black, sewn nose and
mouth; felt paws;
jointed limbs; swivel
head; squeaker; large
head with upturned
nose; thin limbs.
$110

Leaning Bear

Merrythought's "Beefeater"

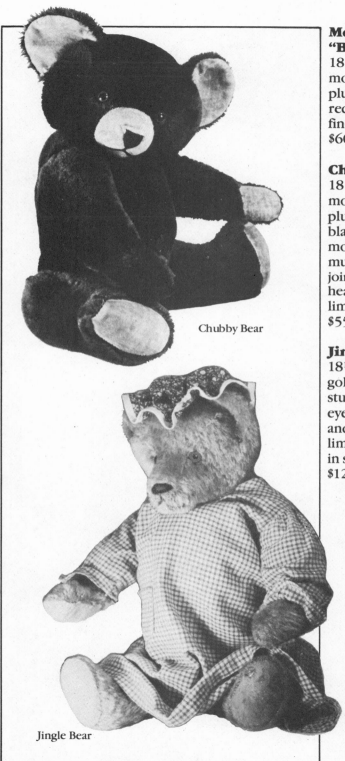

Merrythought's "Beefeater"
18 inches; modern; English; plush; Beefeater outfit red with gold trim; finest quality.
$60

Chubby Bear
18 inches; modern; dark brown plush; soft stuffed; black, sewn nose and mouth; velvet paws, muzzle and ear linings; jointed limbs; swivel head; pudgy torso and limbs.
$55

Chubby Bear

Jingle Bear
18½ inches; gold mohair; straw stuffed; glass stickpin eyes; black, sewn nose and mouth; jointed limbs; swivel head; bell in stomach; hump.
$125

Jingle Bear

Friendly Bear

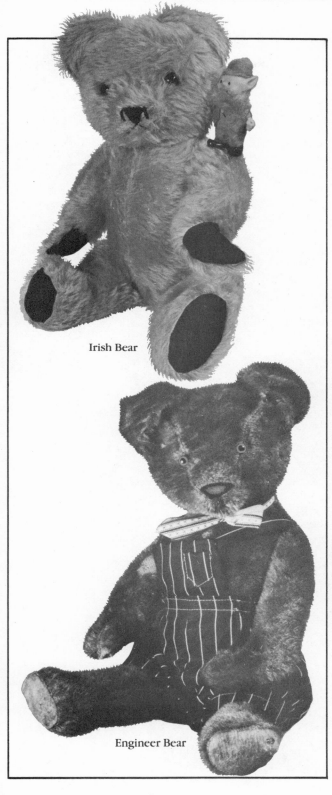

Irish Bear

Engineer Bear

Friendly Bear
19 inches;
circa 1940s; white
mohair; soft stuffed;
glass stickpin eyes;
black, sewn nose and
mouth; felt paws;
jointed limbs; swivel
head; squeaker.
Old White Mohair
Dog: Steiff; straw
stuffed; stickpin eyes;
swivel head; squeaker.
Dog: $65
Bear: $150

Irish Bear
19 inches;
1940s; yellow-gold
mohair; safety
(secured) eyes; black,
sewn nose and mouth;
fabric paws; jointed
limbs; swivel head;
chubby body; "Made
in Republic of Ireland"
on tag.
Leprechaun is from the
1970s and added for
good luck.
Leprechaun: $2
Bear: $95

Engineer Bear
19 inches;
brown mohair; glass
eyes; jointed limbs;
swivel head.
$135 and up

Grizzly Bear

Heart-faced Bear

Grizzly Bear

19 inches;
early 1900s; fluffy gold
mohair; straw stuffed;
glass stickpin eyes;
brown, sewn nose and
mouth; felt paws;
jointed limbs; swivel
head; hump; realistic
appearance; rare.
$250 and up

Heart-faced Bear

19 inches;
circa 1920s; gold
mohair; straw stuffed;
shoe button eyes;
black, sewn nose and
mouth; felt paws;
jointed limbs; swivel
head; squeaker; hump;
unusual expression.
$120-$130

Alert Bear

19 inches;
1920s; gold mohair;
straw stuffed; glass
eyes; black, sewn nose
and mouth; original
felt paws replaced;
jointed limbs; swivel
head; stiff, elongated
torso.
$95

Alert Bear

Clown Bear

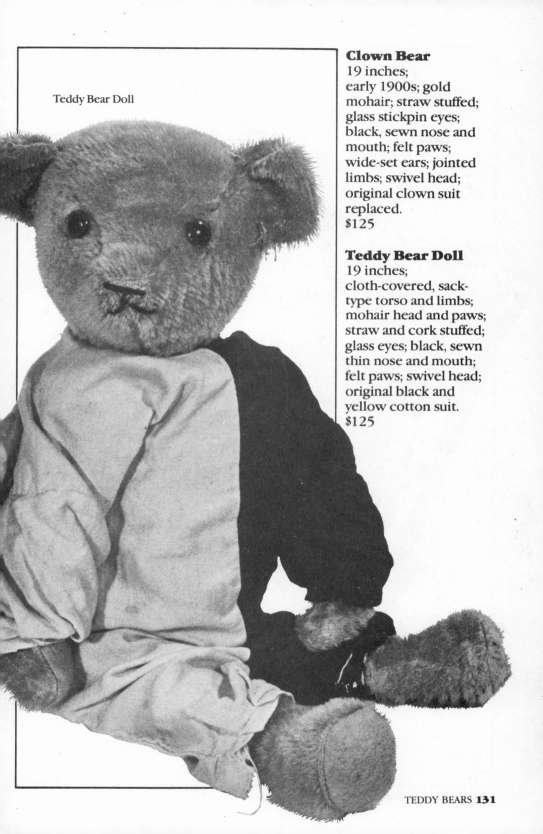

Teddy Bear Doll

Clown Bear
19 inches;
early 1900s; gold
mohair; straw stuffed;
glass stickpin eyes;
black, sewn nose and
mouth; felt paws;
wide-set ears; jointed
limbs; swivel head;
original clown suit
replaced.
$125

Teddy Bear Doll
19 inches;
cloth-covered, sack-
type torso and limbs;
mohair head and paws;
straw and cork stuffed;
glass eyes; black, sewn
thin nose and mouth;
felt paws; swivel head;
original black and
yellow cotton suit.
$125

Inquisitive Bear

Rocking Chair Bear

Inquisitive Bear
19 inches;
1920s; gold mohair;
straw stuffed; glass
stickpin eyes; black,
sewn nose and mouth;
jointed limbs; swivel
head.
$100

Rocking Chair Bear
20 inches;
1920s; Steiff; gold
mohair; straw stuffed;
glass eyes; brown,
sewn nose and mouth;
felt paws; jointed
limbs; swivel head;
squeaker.
$200 and up

Autographed Bear
20 inches;
1970s; English; Peggy
Nisbet; mohair; soft
stuffed; black, sewn
nose and mouth;
jointed limbs; swivel
head; signed;
"Autographed
Collector's Edition"
on tag.
$85

Autographed Bear

Sociable Bear

Literary Bear

Sociable Bear

20 inches; 1920s; gold mohair; straw stuffed; glass stickpin eyes; felt paws; jointed limbs; swivel head. Willow Pattern Doll Tea Set: service for four, plus pot, creamer and sugar bowl in original box.
Tea Set: $65 and up
Bear: $115

Literary Bear

20 inches; early 1900s; brown mohair; straw stuffed; glass eyes; black, sewn nose and mouth; felt paws; jointed limbs; swivel head; exceptional quality. Book: *Der faule Teddybar;* inscription dated 1928; German; color plates.
Book: $55
Bear: $250 and up

Very Important Bear

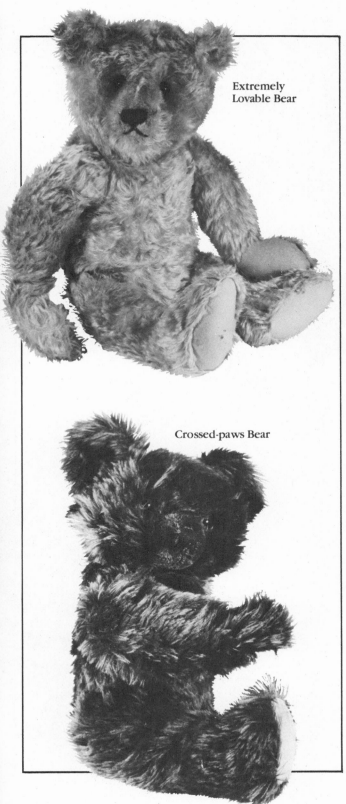

Extremely
Lovable Bear

Crossed-paws Bear

Very Important Bear
20 inches;
early 1900s; Steiff;
silky, light gold mohair;
straw stuffed; large
shoe button eyes;
brown, sewn nose and
mouth; felt paws;
jointed limbs; swivel
head; hump; long arms;
large feet; extremely
appealing; rare in this
size and condition.
$250 and up

Extremely Lovable Bear
20 inches;
Steiff; white mohair;
glass eyes; brown,
sewn nose and mouth;
felt paws; jointed
limbs; swivel head;
deep, low-voiced
squeaker.
$200 and up

Crossed-paws Bear
20 inches;
1938; Knickerbocker;
brown mohair; soft
stuffed; glass eyes;
black, sewn nose and
mouth; velvet paws;
jointed limbs; swivel
head; round face.
$95

Turned-up Nose Bear

Thoughtful Bear

Open-mouth Bear

Nosy Bear

Turned-up Nose Bear
21 inches;
early 1900s; gold
mohair; straw stuffed;
glass stickpin eyes;
black, sewn nose and
mouth; felt paws;
jointed limbs; swivel
head; hump; old brass
chain around neck.
$140

Thoughtful Bear
21 inches;
1930s; gold mohair;
straw stuffed; glass
stickpin eyes; brown,
sewn nose and mouth;
felt paws; jointed
limbs; swivel head;
pear-shaped torso.
$100 and up

Open-mouth Bear
21 inches;
1939-40;
Knickerbocker; brown
mohair; soft stuffed;
glass stickpin eyes;
brown, sewn nose; felt
mouth; felt paws;
jointed limbs; swivel
head; growler in body.
$200

Nosy Bear
21 inches;
circa 1930s; cinnamon
mohair; soft stuffed;
black glass stickpin
eyes; black, sewn nose
and mouth; velvet
paws; jointed limbs;
swivel head; squeaker;
modified hump;
elongated muzzle.
$100

Super Bear

Cinnamon Bear

Hungry Bear

Super Bear
21 inches;
Steiff; gold mohair;
straw stuffed; glass
eyes; black, sewn nose
and mouth; felt paws;
jointed limbs; swivel
head; growler; hump;
finest quality.
$150 and up

Cinnamon Bear
21 inches;
cinnamon mohair;
straw stuffed; shoe
button eyes; brown,
sewn nose and mouth;
felt paws; jointed
limbs; large swivel
head; squeaker; hump;
plump torso and limbs.
$135-$150

Hungry Bear
21 inches;
1930s; light mohair;
soft stuffed; glass eyes;
black, sewn nose and
mouth; felt paws;
jointed limbs; swivel
head; handmade
Teddy Bear bib not
original.
$110

Sailor Bear

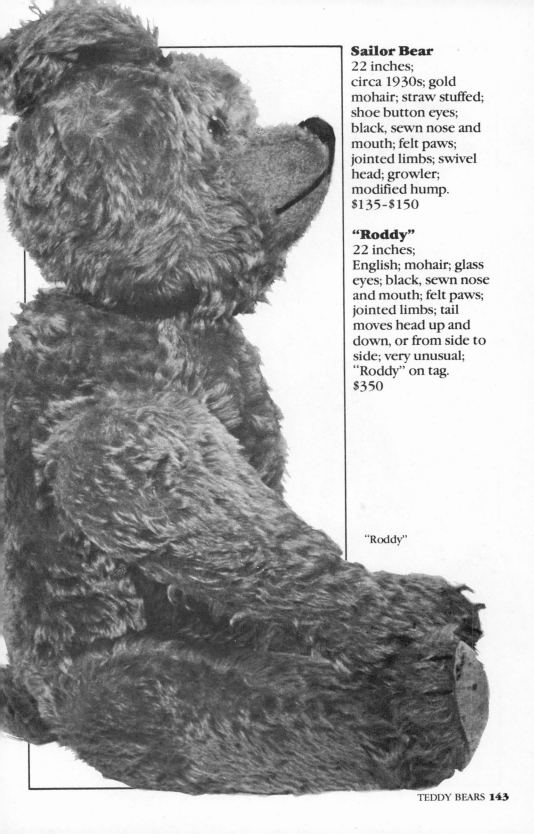

Sailor Bear
22 inches;
circa 1930s; gold
mohair; straw stuffed;
shoe button eyes;
black, sewn nose and
mouth; felt paws;
jointed limbs; swivel
head; growler;
modified hump.
$135-$150

"Roddy"
22 inches;
English; mohair; glass
eyes; black, sewn nose
and mouth; felt paws;
jointed limbs; tail
moves head up and
down, or from side to
side; very unusual;
"Roddy" on tag.
$350

"Roddy"

Baggy Bear

Baggy Bear
23 inches;
early 1900s; mohair;
glass stickpin eyes;
jointed limbs; swivel
head; hump; heart-
shaped face.
$200

Chair Bear
23 inches;
light gold mohair;
straw stuffed; glass
stickpin eyes; fabric
nose; brown, sewn
mouth; replaced paw
felt; jointed limbs;
hump; plump, stiff
body and limbs.
$150

Chair Bear

Frosty Bear

Electric-eye Bear

Large Bear

Battery Bear

Electric-eye Bear
23 inches;
1918-1919; red,
white, and blue
mohair; straw stuffed;
glass bulb eyes; black,
sewn nose and mouth;
jointed at shoulders;
press stomach to
activate battery in
torso which lights up
eyes; unusual.
In working condition:
$200

Frosty Bear
24 inches;
circa 1930s; white
mohair; soft stuffed;
glass eyes; black, sewn
nose; felt paws; jointed
limbs; swivel head;
squeaker.
$175

Large Bear
24 inches;
English; gold mohair;
straw stuffed; glass
stickpin eyes; black,
sewn nose and mouth;
replaced felt paws;
jointed limbs; swivel
head; very chubby
torso, firm to the
touch.
$165

Battery Bear
24 inches;
1918-1919; white;
straw stuffed; jointed
arms; battery pack in
back gives power to
light eye bulbs.
In working condition:
$200

Broad-nosed Bear

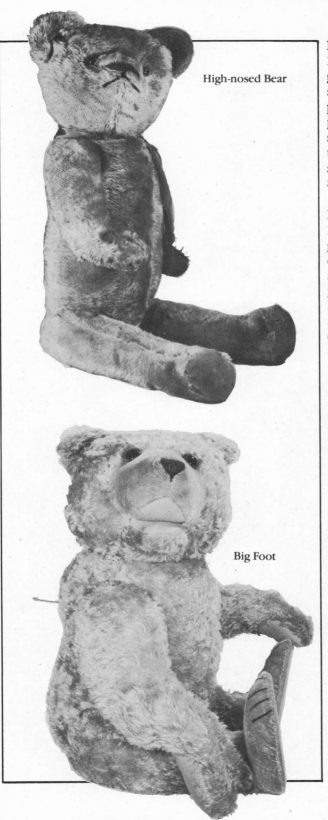

High-nosed Bear

Big Foot

Broad-nosed Bear
24 inches;
gold mohair; glass
stickpin eyes; felt
paws; wide-set ears;
jointed limbs; wide
swivel head; fat torso;
thin limbs with short
arms.
$165

High-nosed Bear
25 inches;
gold mohair; glass
eyes; black, sewn nose
and mouth; felt paws;
jointed limbs; swivel
head; squeaker; short
arms; thin legs; stiff,
elongated torso.
$150

Big Foot
36 inches;
Steiff; light gold
mohair; glass eyes;
brown, sewn nose; felt
open mouth and paws;
jointed limbs; swivel
head; growler
mechanism operated
by wire pulled from
back; hump; "U.S.-
Zone-Germany"
on tag.
$1,200

Four-wheeler

Brown Bear

Nodding Musician

Bears on All Fours

Four-wheeler
8 inches high (including wheels); Steiff; mohair; glass eyes; swivel head; squeaker; metal wheels; tail.
$125

Brown Bear
9 inches high (not including stand); 1930s; dark brown mohair; straw stuffed; glass stickpin eyes; black, sewn nose and mouth; felt paws; hump; tail; original black leather collar.
$55

Nodding Musician
9 inches high; circa 1950s; brown plush; black, sewn nose; felt paws; internal music box moves head in circles when wound.
$25

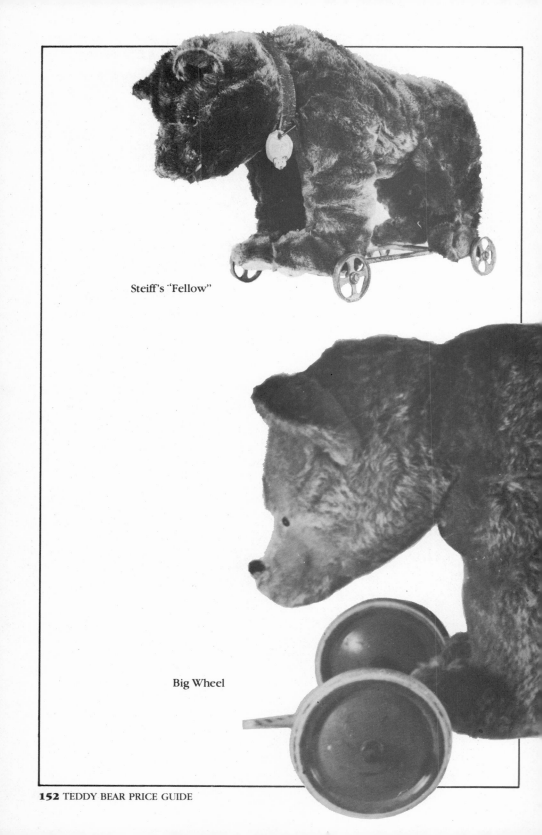

Steiff's "Fellow"

Big Wheel

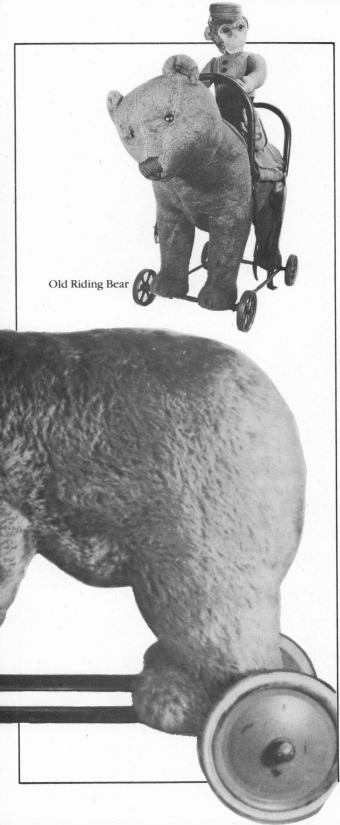

Old Riding Bear

Steiff's "Fellow"
11 inches high (including wheels); dark brown mohair; straw stuffed; glass eyes; felt paws; hump; metal wheels; "Fellow" on tag.
$125

Old Riding Bear
19½ inches (including wheels); early 1900s; brown mohair; shoe button eyes; black, sewn nose and mouth; swivel head; red felt, cloth-lined saddle blanket; leather-covered steel handles on saddle; iron wheels.
Monkey: 14 inches; straw stuffed; glass eyes; sewn-on bellboy red and black felt clothes; felt hands and feet with fingers and toes; jointed limbs; tail moves head.
Monkey: $150
Bear: $375

Big Wheel
20 inches (including wheels); modern; Steiff; brown mohair; straw stuffed; glass eyes; brown, sewn nose; growler operated by pulling heavy wire in back; hump.
In working condition: $250

Old Winnie-the-Pooh

Winnie-the-Pooh

Another
Winnie-the-Pooh

Roly-Poly

Not Quite Teddy Bears

Old Winnie-the-Pooh
6½ inches;
circa 1930s; English;
brown felt; glass eyes;
delicately sewn nose
and mouth; jointed
limbs.
Piglet: 4 inches; circa
1930s; pink felt; glass
eyes; delicately sewn
nose and mouth;
jointed limbs.
Pair: $65

Winnie-the-Pooh
11 inches;
English; soft stuffed;
floppy arms; red sock
hat.
$25

Another Winnie-the-Pooh
13 inches;
1950s-1960s; felt; soft
stuffed; black button
eyes; black felt nose;
stitched-on limbs; with
original red shirt.
$25

Roly-Poly
8 inches;
1970s; Fisher-Price;
plush head and arms;
body soft stuffed over
chimes; fabric muzzle,
ear linings, and paws;
swivel head.
$2

Three Versions of Smokey the Bear

Another Smokey

Three Versions of Smokey the Bear

In 1953, Ideal Toy Corp. was given permission to make and sell Smokey Bear dolls; the company also printed Junior Forest Ranger cards and packed one with each doll. Some 16,000 youngsters applied to be Junior Forest Rangers, and Ideal was honored with a "Golden Smokey" award in 1967 for its contribution.
Left; 12 inches; $15; center; 17 inches; molded face, glass-like eyes, $35; right, 16 inches, $25.

Another Smokey

16 inches;
Talking mechanism; yellow plastic hat; belt reads "Smokey"; ranger badge on chest.
In working condition: $60

Kellogg Bears

Koala

Knickerbocker's
"Yogi Bear"

Kellogg Bears
Three bears, largest is 12 inches; 1920s; fabric printed with red, white, blue, and brown; soft stuffed; company premium; set includes Goldilocks (not pictured). Set of four: $150

Koala
15 inches; modern; Steiff; mohair; felt nose and open mouth; jointed limbs; swivel head; squeaker; legs are bent in curved position; bendable fingers and toes; unique appearance. $150

Knickerbocker's "Yogi Bear"
16 inches; 1959; Hanna-Barbera Productions character made by Knickerbocker; brown plush; soft stuffed; molded face; yellow paws and front; green felt tie. $40

Luggage Carrier, two positions

Luggage Carrier
Modern; battery-operated; switch activates bear to carry suitcases a few steps, turn somersaults, and continue walking.
$15

Panda
24 inches; 1940s; Character; soft stuffed; red felt tongue; floppy limbs.
$55

Panda

Perfume Holder

Compact Bear, two views

Teddy Bear Items

Perfume Holder
1½ inches;
1970s; metal; Teddy
Bear's hinged back
opens to reveal solid
Max Factor perfume.
$20

Compact Bear
3¾ inches;
early 1900s; mohair;
jointed limbs; head is
removed to show
hinged body
containing mirror.
$110

Perfume Bottle
Bear
3¾ inches;
early 1900s; mohair;
black button-type eyes;
black, sewn nose and
mouth; jointed limbs;
head is removed to
show glass perfume
bottle; rare.
$85

Perfume Bottle Bear, three views

Bear Muff

Attentive-bear Muff

Hand Puppet

Bear Muff
14 inches high;
light gold mohair; glass
eyes; black, sewn nose;
muff has quilted lining;
rare.
$250 and up

Attentive-bear Muff
15 inches;
early 1900s; gray
mohair plush; thick
lining; glass eyes;
black, sewn nose; felt
paws; rare.
$250 and up

Hand Puppet
Early 1960s; brown
mohair; Steiff; felt
paws; open mouth.
$20

Bears-You-Wear

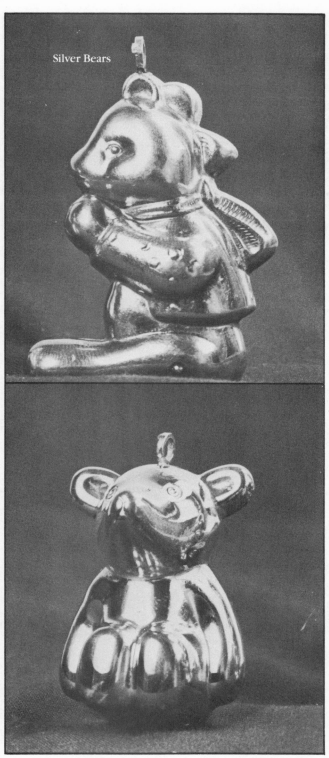

Silver Bears

Bears-You-Wear
Assorted Teddy Bear jewelry, varying in price from $4 (stickpin) to more than $400 (large, jointed charm in center).

Silver Bears
Silver-plated Christmas ornaments can also be worn on neck chains. One on right has hidden bell inside. $15 each

China Bears

China Bears

early 1900s; German; available in many styles and sizes; easily recognizable because of green and white coloring on vase or purse; price varies depending upon appeal and number of animals per piece.
Each: $45 and up

Bisque Bear

Bisque Bear

1¾ inches; probably German; old white bisque; hand-painted face; jointed limbs; hump; fits in old pocket watch; very rare.
$200

Wood Bear

5 inches; 1970s; Danish; jointed at hips and shoulders; swivel head.
$15-20

Baby Rattle

4 inches; plastic; shaped like long-nosed Roosevelt bear.
$2

Wood Bear

Baby Rattle

Climbing Bear, two views

Climbing Bear
6½ inches;
German; mohair; metal
eyes; jointed limbs;
does tricks on 16-inch
wooden stick.
$150

Jack-in-the-Box
8 inches;
Teddy Bear with
parasol; wood handle
turns and plays music
while bear bobs up
and down; rare.
$200

Jack-in-the-Box

Paper Dolls

Paper Dolls
10½-inch Teddy Bear; early 1900s; E.I. Horsman; paper; five outfits; two hats; original paper envelope.
$350

Old Coffee Service
Lithographed tin; Teddies on tray, cups, pot.
$85

New Coffee Service
1970s; German; plastic; doll dishes with Teddy motif.
$6

Old Coffee Service

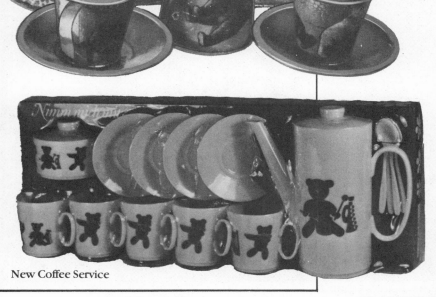

New Coffee Service

New Bears

The following section is devoted to newer bears. The ones selected to appear on these pages were chosen because of their quality, appeal, or possible future collectibility. A few were picked because they had unusual features.

The examples shown are only a part of the wide variety of wonderful modern Teddy Bears from which you may make your choices. Because prices vary from store to store throughout the country we have not included them. The importance of these bears is their potential value as a collectible. But, contemporary manufacturers and designers are offering creations so cuddly and cheerful, that it shouldn't matter whether or not some of them become collectible—they make irresistible companions.

H2W's "Bear Claus"

Although a few modern bears are covered with mohair, many are made with man-made plush fabrics. Stuffing materials are also modern, since safety regulations and practices find straw and excelsior to be too flammable.

In most cases, these bears have shatterproof eyes securely fastened into their heads, since glass stickpin eyes are also considered too hazardous for young children. Some bears have features which are dyed or molded rather than embroidered.

Although these bears were available at the time of publication, if you have difficulty finding any you would like to own, consult the directory on page 214, for the manufacturer's or importer's address and telephone number. Some, however, may have been discontinued.

New Bear Guide

H2W's "Bear Claus"
18 inches;
complete with stuffed reindeer and wooden sleigh; irresistible Christmas display.

Steiff's "Petsy"
8 inches;
tan plush; soft stuffed; brown, sewn nose and mouth; fully jointed; swivel head; cute expression.

Steiff's "Petsy"

Dollhouse Bears

Snappy Bear

Easily-led Teddy

Dollhouse Bears
3½ inches;
German; Schuco;
jointed limbs; well
made; price includes
clothes, specially made
and available through
Enchanted Doll House;
becoming hard to find.

Snappy Bear
4 inches;
Chinese; cotton
corduroy; limbs snap
on and off; head ribbon
used for hanging bear.

Easily-led Teddy
5 inches high;
German; Hermann;
caramel-colored
mohair; swivel head;
red collar with gold
metal tag; finest
quality.

Polish Bears

Steiff's "Rattler"

French Bear

Polish Bears
7 inches and 11 inches;
1970s; Polish; tan or dark brown plush; soft stuffed; jointed limbs.

Steiff's "Rattler"
8 inches (including wheels);
plush; still available in some stores; pull toy; cute.

French Bear
9 inches;
French; unusual chintz fabric has silky feel; smiling; pot-bellied; handmade; "Mikkie Malsan . . . Petit Faune" on label. Available through LMS Imports.

Bumblebee Surprise, four views

Berenstain Bear

Mattel's "Lullaby Bear"

Bumblebee Surprise

Zippersnapper™ by Jodi Bauernschmidt, Gadzooks Toys; bee mouth unzips; stuffing pulls out; bumblebee fits into open mouth of—what else?—a Teddy Bear.

Berenstain Bear

10 inches; Knickerbocker Toy Co.; stuffed version of cartoon bears in the Berenstains' children's books; available in two sizes; other characters also available.

Mattel's "Lullaby Bear"

11 inches; Love Notes Pets series; brown plush with white paws and brown and white ears; molded face; bear plays musical tunes when colored circles are pressed.

British Bear

British Bear

11 inches;
English; light blue
plush; soft stuffed;
glass-like plastic eyes;
black, sewn nose and
mouth; "Wendy
Boston, made in
England" on label.

Hasbro's "Teri Teddy"

11 inches;
terrycloth; "1972,
Hasbro Industries Inc."
on tag.

Bear on right

12 inches;
German; Käthe Kruse;
brown plush; available
in terrycloth.

Hasbro's "Teri Teddy"   Bear on right

Rock-A-Bye-Baby's "Rock-A-Bye-Bear"

On the tag: Rock-A-Bye-Bear with the ROCK·A·BYE BABY SOUND

Determined Productions'
"Joshua Bear"

Playmate

Eden's "Paddingtons"

**Rock-A-Bye-Baby's
"Rock-A-Bye-Bear"**
11½ inches;
light yellow plush;
audio unit run by 9-
volt battery reached
through velcro slot in
bottom of bear;
"Rock-A-Bye-Baby,
Inc., Ft. Lauderdale,
Florida, 1975" on tag.
Accompanying
brochure reads:
"Contains actual
maternal pulse sounds
as heard by baby in the
womb..."

**Determined
Productions'
"Joshua Bear"**
11 inches;
light brown plush;
variety of clothes
available;
"Determined
Productions, Inc.
1979" on tag.
Playmate
6½ inches;
Determined
Productions; light
brown plush; no
clothes.

**Eden's
"Paddingtons"**
12 inches and 18
inches (including
hats);
brown plush with
darker paws; "Eden
Toys, Inc., New York,
N.Y." on tag; available
in a variety of sizes and
outfits.

Pot Belly Bear
and Friend

H2W's "Colonel Teddy"

Colonel Teddy

The Teddy Roosevelt Bear

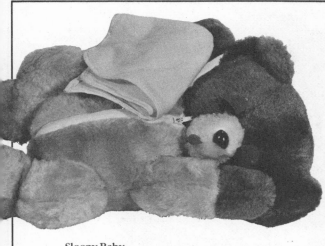

Sleepy Baby

Pot Belly Bear's Friend (on left):
12 inches; light brown plush; cream-colored muzzle and paws; "Miss Boutique, N.Y.C." on tag.

Pot Belly Bear
18 inches; light brown plush; cream-colored muzzle and paws; "Daekor Designs Div., Hudson Bay Trading Company, Ltd. New York," on tag. (Company now Hudson Brands Trading Company, Ltd.)

Sleepy Baby
12½ inches; Enesco Imports Corp.; bear cub with sleepy eyes; molded plastic nose; red felt tongue; swivel head; working zipper on non-removable drop-seat pajamas; security blanket; cute and unusual.

H2W's "Colonel Teddy"
14 inches; brown plush with velvet-like paws and ears; available in colonel's blue uniform, Rough Rider khaki or presidential tux; comes complete with storybook and wire specs.

Muppet's "Fozzie Bear"

College Bear

Reuge Bear

Muppet's "Fozzie Bear"
14 inches; orange-brown plush; thumbs on paws; pink nose; pink polka-dot tie; brown hat; "Fisher-Price Toys and Henson Associates, Inc. 1976" on tag.

College Bear
14 inches; tan plush; felt feet; felt hat; complete with "D" for Dartmouth sweater; available in sweaters with other college letters; "Telemarks, Inc., New Hampshire" on tag.

Reuge Bear
14 inches; Swiss; quality brown plush; black, sewn nose and mouth; felt paws; jointed limbs; wind-up movement turns head while bear plays "The Teddy Bear's Picnic." Available through Fagan International.

Merrythought's New "Cheeky"

Freemountain's "Emile Bearheart"

Italian Bear

Merrythought's New "Cheeky"
14 inches; English; light gold mohair blend; felt paws; wide-set ears; jointed limbs; swivel head; unique happy expression; classic fine quality; "Merrythought, Ironbridge, Shrops., Made in England" on tag on foot.

Freemountain's "Emile Bearheart"
Plush; paws with thumbs; stuffed red heart; two pockets; handmade; machine washable.

Italian Bear
15 inches; Italy; Lenci; mink-like plush; finest quality; with Lenci certificate; available in other sizes.

Treasure Bear

Heart-nosed Bear

100th Anniversary Bear

Treasure Bear
16 inches;
Princess Soft Toys; a
cuddly classic;
available in other sizes.

Heart-nosed Bear
16½ inches;
light brown plush;
elongated muzzle with
heart-shaped appliqué;
chubby and cute;
"Animal Fair, Inc.
1975" on tag. Plastic
Teddy Bear picnic
basket by Fisher-Price.

100th Anniversary
Bear
17 inches;
Steiff commemorative
(1880-1980); limited
edition of 11,000;
numbered ear tag;
reproduction of the
1903 original; mohair;
jointed limbs; swivel
head; includes special
box and official signed
certificate.

Ballerina-at-the-Barre

H2W's "Basic Brown Bear" (B.B. Bear)

Knitted French Bear

Ballerina-at-the-Barre

17 inches; German; Hermann; finest quality mohair; jointed limbs; growler; tutu, real ballet slippers, and barre were added.

H2W'S "Basic Brown Bear" (B.B. Bear)

17 inches; brown plush; soft stuffed; plastic eyes; black felt nose; black, sewn mouth; floppy limbs; variety of clothes available.

Knitted French Bear

18 inches; French; knitted on design of green trousers and suspenders, fastened with tan buttons; embroidered face; fabric-covered button nose; "Mikkie Malsan . . . Petit Faune" on label. Available through LMS Imports.

Handmade Bears

Swiss Bear

Chinese Bear

Singing Bear

Handmade Bears
18 inches;
Diane Babb; dark
brown plush; jointed
limbs; swivel heads;
exceptional quality
(bear-printed shirts
are not original).

Swiss Bear
18 inches;
felt paws; jointed
limbs; swivel head;
hump; fine quality;
"Felpa ... Zurich ...
Mutzli" on tag;
available in other sizes.

Chinese Bear
18 inches;
light gold, pure wool
plush; felt paws;
jointed limbs;
elongated muzzle;
antique appearance;
"S.D.F. (Shanghai Dolls
Factory), made in
China" on tag;
available in other sizes.

Singing Bear
19 inches;
German; removable
record plays a German
Teddy Bear song on
one side and has
German phrases on the
other; super bear.
Available through
Fagan International.

Floppy Bear

Floppy Bear
20 inches;
German; Käthe Kruse;
beige, woolly-looking
plush; black button
eyes and nose.
Available in other
colors.

**North American
Bear Co.'s
"Running Bear"**
20 inches;
brown plush; very
unusual; well made;
wears red jersey
jogging suit and white
track shoes; "North
American Bear
Company, designed by
Barbara Isenberg" on
tag.

North American Bear
Co.'s "Running Bear"

Valentine Bear

Valentine Bear
24 inches; Atlanta Novelty, division of Gerber Products Company; white Polar Bear; "Be My Valentine" on tag.

Possum Trot's "UFB" (Unidentified Flying Bear)
24 inches; designed by Gillian Bradshaw-Smith; space suit; pack straps to back; removable helmet.

Possum Trots' "UFB" (Unidentified Flying Bear)

Dakin's "Bearfoot"
25 inches; light brown plush; unusual paws with individual toes; exceptionally appealing and popular; "Pillow Pets, R. Dakin & Company, San Francisco, California, 1976" on tag; available in a variety of sizes and colors.

Dakin's "Bearfoot"

Big Things To Do With Little Bears

Miniature bears are usually thought of as those six inches high or less. The smaller they are, the more fun you can have displaying them.

Use props. Let these bears become incorporated into your favorite decor. If they are small enough, many Teddy Bears can be displayed in dollhouses or simply on dollhouse furniture—old or new. Because dollhouses are now important as collectibles, miniaturia, as the hobby is called, has produced an endless array of wonderful objects and habitats suitable for discriminating Teddy Bear owners.

Search dollhouse and craft shops for bargains. Houses come in conventional models as well as Victorian mansions. There are log cabins, townhouses, Cape Cods—you name it.

The most fun is finding treasures to put inside these houses. There is no limit. Any object you

German Wood Fort

have in your home or office is already available in miniature. Search them out at the miniaturia shows which are open to the public. Plus, if you are skilled at do-it-yourself projects, there are special tools and materials available, as well as kits of everyday items and even museum reproductions.

Miniaturia can be an overwhelming hobby with prices on tempting items running anywhere from a few cents for a little dinner plate to thousands of dollars for a pre-finished, lighted dollhouse. There is no need to spend a lot of money, though. You can have a great deal of fun using whatever you find around the house. The scenes pictured in these pages vary in decor from modern leftovers to museum-quality antiques. They all, however, have one major thing in common—they're innovative, comfortable and, in many cases, luxurious enough to allow your Teddy Bears to live in the style to which you yourself would like to be accustomed.

Miniaturia

German Wood Fort
27 x 21 x 19 inches; 1930s; buildings and bridges store in base compartment.

Red Double-deck Bus
23 x 12 x 7 inches; 1940s; steel; Scottish. Modern Steiff Teddy Bears and Pandas act as riders.

Red Double-deck Bus

High Chair

Dining Room Set

High Chair
Wood; slide-out tray on swivel. Modern bear, 4½ inches, waits to be fed.

Dining Room Set
Old Steiff bears take tea.

Wagon
Early 1900s; wood; hand-painted Teddy inscription on side. Old Steiff bears ride inside.

Wagon

Rugs and Pennants

Hand-decorated Goose Egg,
two views

Rugs and Pennants
Circa 1920s; old
cigarette "felts,"
premiums offered by
cigarette companies.

**Hand-decorated
Goose Egg**
Hinged; opens to
reveal an old wood
Teddy Bear instead of
the Easter Bunny.

Playskool Pullman Train Car, two views

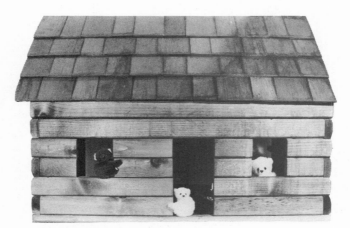

Rustic Log Cabin, two views

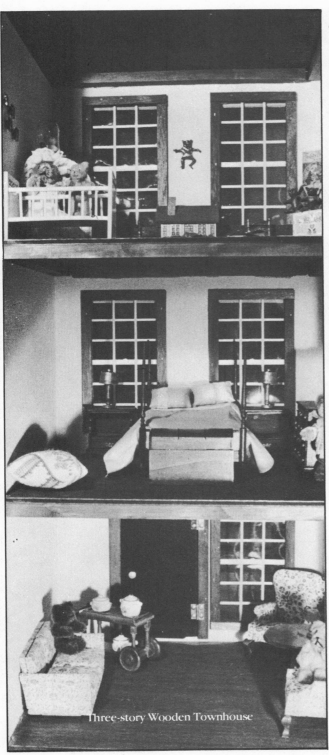

Three-story Wooden Townhouse

Playskool Pullman Train Car
12 x 10 x 5 inches; early 1930s; tin; believed to be one of only one hundred ever produced; interior includes original curtains, pillows, sheets, blankets, table, berth, and closet.

Rustic Log Cabin
26 x 14 x 24 inches; perfect home for novelty "clip-on" bears.

Three-story Wooden Townhouse
13 x 13 x 29 inches; illustrated model serves as end table.

Dollhouse Living Room Set

Lounge

Red Fire Engine

Tree-house Condo,
two views

Dollhouse Living Room Set
Old; velvet; non-scale. Old Steiff bears, 3½ inches, complete the scene.

Lounge
New velvet; inch-to-a-foot scale. Old bisque bears are seated on the lounge.

Red Fire Engine
Once housed inexpensive liqueur set; Steiff bears replaced bottles; Steiff horse added for power. The whole team fits on a mantel.

Tree-house Condo
26½ inches high; German; wood tree-trunk dollhouse; hinged; three floors (furniture and bears pictured are not original); when new, carried in U.S. by F.A.O. Schwarz, New York, exclusively.

Directory

Attentive Bear
(See page 95)

Directory

The following directory is a partial but representative listing of manufacturers, importers, distributors, retailers, clubs, specialists, and periodicals that are related to or include Teddy Bears. This is not intended to be a complete list but solely a starting point for the collector. *Although it isn't specifically mentioned, each manufacturer, importer and distributor listed carries Teddy Bears, and usually other soft toys.* Any other information of interest is described with each entry. As you add your own information to the directory, you can increase its value and scope by aiming it in the direction you wish your own hobby to take.

Manufacturers, Importers, Distributors

Animal Fair, Inc.
P.O. Box 1326
Minneapolis, Minn. 55440
(612) 831-7200

Art's Toy Manufacturing Company
P.O. Box 116
600 W. Main Street
Pen Argyl, Pa. 18072
(215) 863-4164

Atlanta Novelty Manufacturing Corp.
(Division of Gerber Products Co.)
1911 Park Avenue
New York, N.Y. 10035
(212) 392-8505

Russ Berrie & Company, Inc.
111 Bauer Drive
Oakland, N.J. 07436
(201) 891-7500

Wallace Berrie & Co., Inc.
7628 Densmore Avenue
Van Nuys, Ca. 91406
(213) 787-2700
Ceramic Teddy Bears

Brooklyn Doll
30 Waverly Avenue
Brooklyn, N.Y. 11205
(212) 522-4118

California Stuffed Toys
611 S. Anderson Street
Los Angeles, Ca. 90023
(213) 268-8381

Chinchilla Furs, Inc.
22 Purchase Street
Rye, N.Y. 10580
(914) 967-8370
Soft, real fur animal toys

R. Dakin & Company
499 Pt. San Bruno Boulevard
S. San Francisco, Ca. 94080
(415) 952-1777

Davis-Grabowski, Inc.
74 N.E. 74 Street
Miami, Fla. 33138
(305) 751-3667

Deans Childsplay Toys Ltd.
Pontnewynydd
Pontypool, Gwent
United Kingdom NP4 6YY
Pontypool 4881/2 (Stdcode 04955)

Determined Productions, Inc.
Box 2150
San Francisco, Ca. 94126
(415) 433-0660
Teddy Bears; Teddy Bear clothes

Douglas Co., Inc.
Krif Road
Keene, N.H. 03431
(603) 352-3414

Enesco Imports Corp.
2201 Arthur Avenue
Elk Grove Village, Ill. 60007
(312) 640-5200
*Teddy Bears; other soft toys;
ceramics; other items*

Fagan International
1843 Business Center Drive
Duarte, Ca. 91010
(213) 286-7072
*Teddy Bear imports including
German Singing Bear, Käthe Kruse,
Reuge Musical Bear; Merrythought,
Hermann, and others*

Fisher-Price Toys
(Division of The Quaker Oats Co.)
620 Girard Avenue
East Aurora, N.Y. 14052
(800) 828-1440

Freemountain Toys, Inc.
23 Main Street
Bristol, Vt. 05443
(802) 453-2462

Gund Manufacturing Co.
44 National Road
Edison, N.J. 08817
(201) 287-0880
*Luv-Me Bear; Winnie-the-Pooh;
other Teddy Bears*

H2W, Inc.
834 Mission Street
San Francisco, Ca. 94103
(415) 543-6058

**Hudson Brands Trading
Co., Ltd.**
41 Madison Avenue
New York, N.Y. 10010
(212) 686-1440
Pot Belly Bear

Ideal Toy Corporation
184-10 Jamaica Avenue
Hollis, N.Y. 11423
(212) 454-5000; 675-6100
*Made original Teddy Bears; 75th
anniversary bear; Smokey Bears;
other bears; dolls; toys; games*

Importoys, Inc.
3364 S. Robertson Boulevard
Los Angeles, Ca. 90034
(213) 837-4477
*Teddy Bear imports; other
soft toys*

Kamar International, Inc.
23639 Hawthorne Boulevard
Torrance, Ca. 90505
(213) 378-5216

Charleen Kinser Designs
R.D. 1, Box 488
Boalsburg, Pa. 16827
(814) 466-7846

Knickerbocker Toy Co., Inc.
1107 Broadway
New York, N.Y. 10010
New Jersey: (201) 752-6900
New York: (212) 741-1300

Koala 'T' Toys, Inc.
3605 Woodhead Drive
Northbrook, Ill. 60062
(312) 291-1190

LMS Imports, Inc.
(Formerly Happily Ever After)
15432 Cabrito Road
Van Nuys, Ca. 91406
(213) 785-1141
Unusual Teddy Bear imports
(Lenci, Felpa, Käthe Kruse, Mikkie
Malsan)

Mattel Toys
5150 Rosecrans Avenue
Hawthorne, Ca. 90250
(213) 644-0411

Merrythoughts Limited
Iron-Bridge
Telford, Shropshire
England TF8 7NJ
Ironbridge (0952-45) 3116

Mary Meyer of Vermont
Mary Meyer Station
Townshend, Vt. 05353
(802) 365-7793

Mighty Star, Inc.
925 Amboy Avenue
Perth Amboy, N.J. 08861
(201) 826-5200

North American Bear Co., Inc.
(Barbara Isenberg)
30 Leroy Street
New York, N.Y. 10014
New York: (212) 989-7269
Chicago: (312) 943-1055
Teddy Bears; special character bears

Patmar Corporation
2300 Payne Avenue
Cleveland, Oh. 44114
(216) 566-9227
Teddy Bear imports; other soft toys;
ceramic Teddy Bear Christmas
tree ornaments; planters

Possum Trot Corporation
P.O. Box 249
McKee, Ky. 40447
(606) 287-8361

Princess Soft Toys
1101 N. 4 Street
Cannon Falls, Minn. 55009
(507) 263-3317

Reeves International, Inc.
(U.S. representative of Margarete
Steiff GmbH)
1107 Broadway
New York, N.Y. 10010
(212) 929-5412
Steiff anniversary bears; Teddy
Bears; other soft toys

The Rushton Company
1275 Ellsworth Ind. Dr.
Atlanta, Ga. 30325
(404) 355-9220

B. Shackman & Co.
(Mail Order Department: Federal
Smallwares) 85 Fifth Avenue
New York, N. Y. 10003
(212) 989-5162
Teddy Bears; other soft toys;
miniaturia; retail and mail order

Philip Stahl Inc.
10 First Street
Pelham, N.Y.
(914) 738-2222

**Stahlwood Toy Manufacturing
Co., Inc.**
601 West 50 Street
New York, N.Y. 10028
(212) 246-5208

Star Merchandise Co., Inc.
11136 Chandler Boulevard
N. Hollywood Ca. 91601
(213) 769-4211
Teddy Bears; imports for carnival
and premium use

Margarete Steiff GmbH
Postfach 1260, D-7928
Giengen/Brenz
West Germany
0-73-22-1311

Tom Taormina
c/o J.P.T. Industries, Inc.
52-54 72 Street
Maspeth, N.Y. 11378
(212) 424-1733

Telemarks, Inc.
123 Main Street
Plaistow, N.H. 03865
(603) 382-8946
*Stuffed toy mascots (including
Teddy Bears)*

Tower Treasures Ltd.
(Peggy Nisbet Teddy Bears)
11 Pembroke Road
Clifton, Bristol
England BS8 3AU

Trudy Toys Co., Inc.
35 Lois Street
Norwalk, Conn. 06856
(203) 846-2005

Retailers

Animal Accents
56 E. Walton Street
Chicago, Ill. 60611
(312) 787-5446
New bears; antique bears

Bear-In-Mind (Fran Lewis)
73 Indian Pipe Lane,
Concord, Mass. 01742
(617) 369-5987
Mail order specialty catalog

The Bear Necessities:
Faneuil Hall Marketplace
Boston, Mass. 02109
(617) 227-2327

Beachwood Place
26300 Cedar Road
Beachwood, Oh. 44122
(216) 464-6342

Freight House Shops
Station Square
Pittsburgh, Pa. 15219
(412) 232-0667

215 Goddard Row
Brick Marketplace
Newport, R.I. 02840
(401) 846-9035
New Bears; other related items

Bear With Us
(Lillian Rohaly)
1532 S. Bentley Avenue
Los Angeles, Ca. 90025
(213) 478-5969
*Antique and new bears; other
related items; other soft toys. Mail
order, wholesale, and shows only*

Bears, Etc.
(Kate and Barbara Blair)
93 Main Street
Cold Spring Harbor, N.Y. 11724
(516) 367-9034
New bears, other related items

Bears in the Wood, Inc.
(Janee Lutticken)
59 N. Santa Cruz Avenue
Los Gatos, Ca. 95030
(408) 354-6974
Bears from around the world

**Bronner's Christmas
Decorations**
25 Christmas Lane
Frankenmuth, Mich. 48734
(517) 652-9931
New bears; other soft toys

Brown-Trump Antiques
(Ed Brown and Ross Trump)
321 N. Court Street
Medina, Oh. 44256
(216) 723-4730
*Antique bears; related antique
items; other antique soft toys*

Gene and Jo Sue Coppa
20 E. Woodhaven Drive
Avon, Conn. 06001
(203) 673-3722
Antique bears

Dollhouse World
(Jean Schroeder)
20391 Miller Avenue
Euclid, Oh. 44119
(216) 486-6664
New and antique miniaturia

Enchanted Doll House
(Barbara Haviland, president)
Route 7
Manchester Center, Vt. 05255
Shop: (802) 362-1327
Mail Order Department:
(802) 362-3030
New bears; other soft toys; also miniaturia

Federal Smallwares
(See B. Shackman & Co.—
Manufacturers' Listing)

Gambucci/Our Own Hardware
1312 E. 13 Avenue
Hibbing, Minn. 55746
(218) 263-3480
New bears; other soft toys

The Glass Rooster
(Jean and John Kehl)
3709 Sixth Avenue
P.O. Box 7001
Tacoma, Wash. 98407
(206) 752-7347
New bears; bear boxes; wardrobes; houses

Hobbitat, Inc.
5717 Xerxes Avenue North
Minneapolis, Minn. 55430
(612) 560-8188
New bears; other soft toys

Ruth Kalb
5958 Ridge Road
Wadsworth, Oh. 44281
(216) 239-1409
Antique bears; antique soft toys

Natalie Kolliner Kutz
Route 2, Box 151
Lake Crystal, Minn. 56055
(507) 947-3785
New and antique bears; other Steiff soft toys

Wanda Loukides
4 Glenwood Drive
Napa, Ca. 94558
(707) 226-3497
New imported bears

Mary Jane's Dolls
(Don and Mary Jane Poley)
9318 Wilson Mills Road
Chesterland, Oh. 44026
(216) 729-7179
Antique bears; antique dolls; other antique soft toys

Nims Sportsmans of Ames
225 Main Street
Ames, Ia. 50010
(515) 232-1482
New bears; other soft toys

Bonnie Rowlands
531 E. Liberty Street
Medina, Oh. 44256
(216) 725-5982
Antique bears; antique soft toys

F.A.O. Schwarz
745 Fifth Avenue
New York, N.Y. 10022
(212) 644-9400
New bears; related items; other soft toys

Shirley's Dollhouse
(Shirley Bertrand)
P.O. Box 99A
971 N. Milwaukee Avenue
Wheeling, Ill. 60090
(312) 537-1632
New and antique bears; other soft toys; bear repair

Sugar Hill
P.O. Box 68
Novelty, Oh. 44072
(216) 338-5212
Antique bears; houses; related
items; bear repair

Taggart's Toys and Hobbies
11 N. Franklin Street
Chagrin Falls, Oh. 44022
(216) 247-5695
New bears; other soft toys;
miniaturia

Taylors Toys
1216 Main Street
Great Bend, Kan. 67530
(316) 793-9698
New bears; other soft toys

Ted E. Bear and Company
Pier 39, G-1
San Francisco, Ca. 94133
(415) 421-1398
New bears; other items

Toy Box Antiques
(Pat Garthoeffner)
Route 1, Box 20
Wentzville, Mo. 63385
(314) 327-8089
Antique bears; other antique soft
toys; rag dolls; Steiff animals; folk
art toys

The Toy Store
709 Kansas Avenue
Topeka, Kan. 66603
(913) 235-0651
New bears; other soft toys

Toys Ahoy (Shop No. 1)
28 Periwinkle Place
Sanibel Island, Fla. 33957
Michigan Office Phone:
(313) 421-6000
New bears, other soft toys

Toys and Treasures
Morgan's Alley
515 S.W. Broadway
Portland, Ore. 97205
(503) 227-1999
New bears; related items; other
soft toys

Toys by Roy
777 Towne East Square
7700 E. Kellogg Street
Wichita, Kan. 67207
(316) 686-4921
New bears; other soft toys

Toyworks
Office and Wholesale:
318 W. 48th Street
Minneapolis, Minn. 55409
(612) 822-8504

Retail Stores:
100 N. Sixth Street
Minneapolis, Minn. 55403
(612) 332-4830

3515 West 69 Street
Edina, Minn. 55435
(612) 922-7505

1511 Plymouth Road
Minnetonka, Minn. 55343
(612) 545-2753
New bears

Wind Bells Cottage Antiques
(Delma Royce Peery)
720 Eighth Street
Hermosa Beach, Ca. 90254
(213) 374-1582
New and antique bears; large
variety of related bear items; other
soft toys; also miniaturia

Winnie's Toy Orphanage
2401 Harding Road
Des Moines, Ia. 50310
(515) 277-6175
New bears; other soft toys

World of Toys and Hobbies
Conestoga Mall
Grand Island, Neb. 68801
(308) 384-5610
New bears; other soft toys

Clubs

Good Bears of the World
P.O. Box 8236
Honolulu, Hi. 96815
(808) 946-2844

Teddy Bear Boosters
P.O. Box 814
Redlands, Ca. 92373

Twin Cities Teddy Bear Club
254 W. Sidney Street
St. Paul, Minn. 55107
(612) 291-7571

Bear Specialists

Jodi Bauernschmidt
Gadzooks Toys (Maker of
Zippersnappers™)
14B Central Street
Woodstock, Vt. 05091
*Bumble bee/Teddy Bear; frog/
prince; silk purse/pig; other
inside-out toys*

Lois Beck
10300 S.E. Champagne Lane
Portland, Ore. 97266
(503) 777-2131
*Teddy Bear stationery; handmade
Teddy Bears, some with bisque
faces; other original items*

Dorothy E. Bordeaux
Route 2, Box 760
Silver Springs, Fla. 32688
(904) 625-1307
*Handmade jointed and
unjointed Teddy Bears*

Kay Bransky
R.D. 2, Box 130
Breinigsville, Pa. 18031
(215) 285-6180
*Teddy Bear stationery; buttons;
postcards; and handmade Teddy
Bears*

Irma Cohen
23 Ledge Road
Gloucester, Mass. 01930
(617) 283-5593
*Unique handmade bear houses
in all sizes; handmade miniature
furniture and needlepoint rugs*

Janna Joseph
Box 9423
Daytona Beach, Fla. 32020
(904) 255-9610
*Jointed porcelain miniature
Teddy Bears*

Jeanne Miller
24 Canter Lane
Sherwood, Ore. 97140
(503) 625-5221
Lecturer on Teddy Bears

Beverly Port
P.O. Box 711
Retsil, Wash. 98378
(206) 871-1633
*Handmade bears, dolls, musicals,
and muffs; authentic fabrics;
authentic eyes, porcelain faces*

Scollon Productions, Inc.
3619 Walton Avenue
Cleveland, Oh. 44113
(216) 671-4510; 631-5777
*Designers and manufacturers of
full size and larger Teddy Bear
costumes, complete with head,
hands, and feet, suitable for
amusement parks, department
stores and other displays.*

Teddy Bear's Boutique
(Sunnie Henry)
Route 3, Box 3180
Selah, Wash. 98942
(509) 697-7773
Original quilt patterns; pillows;
toys, and cards

Karen Walter
304 S.E. 87 Street
Portland, Ore. 97216
(503) 256-4563
Handmade Teddy Bears in variety
of fabrics

Carol-Lynn Rossel Waugh
5 Morrill Street
Winthrop, Me. 04364
(207) 377-6769
Miniature (under 5 inches) jointed
porcelain Teddy Bears and dolls

Marlene Wendt
5935 Lyndale Avenue North
Minneapolis, Minn. 55430
(612) 561-6196
Teddy Bear rubber stamps

Publications

The Antiquarian Magazine
of New York
Box 798
Huntington, N.Y. 11743
(516) 271-8990

Antique Toy World
3941 Belle Plaine
Chicago, Ill. 60618
(312) 725-0633

Antique Trader Weekly
Babka Publishing Co.
Box 1050
100 Bryant Street
Dubuque, Ia. 52001
(319) 588-2073

Antiques and the Arts Weekly
The Bee Publishing Co.
Newtown, Conn. 06470
(203) 426-3141

Antiques & Collectibles
230 Arlington Circle
East Hills, N.Y. 11548
(516) 484-4477

Antiques World Magazine
Artnews
122 E. 42 Street
New York, N.Y. 10017
(212) 599-6060

Bear Tracks
c/o Good Bears of the World
P.O. Box 8236
Honolulu, Hi. 96815
(808) 946-2844

Bernice's Bambini
P.O. Box 33
Highland, Ill. 62249
(618) 675-3497

Hobbies, The Magazine
for Collectors
1006 S. Michigan Avenue
Chicago, Ill. 60605
(312) 939-4767

Kovels on Antiques and
Collectibles
Antiques, Inc.
P.O. Box 22200
Beachwood, Oh. 44122
(216) 831-5100

Playthings
Geyer-McAllister Publications
51 Madison Avenue
New York, N.Y. 10010
(212) 689-4411

The Teddy Tribune
c/o Barbara Wolters
254 W. Sidney Street
St. Paul, Minn. 55107
(612) 291-7571

Tri-State Trader
P.O. Box 90
27 North Jefferson
Knightstown, Ind. 46148
News: (317) 345-5134
Advertising: (317) 345-5800

Catalog Authors and Staff

Peggy and Alan Bialosky live in Ohio, are pet editors for the *Cleveland Plain Dealer,* and authors of *Pets I've Met* and *Teddy Bears.* For over fifteen years they have closely followed the growth of the antique Teddy Bear market, interviewing collectors and researching bears. They are shown here with, from left to right: CB, the twins, Muffy, Anna, Sleeper, Alexander Graham Bear, and Cliffy.